It's Better in America

IT'S BETTER IN AMERICA

A Book of Superlatives

by

PATRICK MAHONY

THE INSTITUTE FOR THE STUDY OF MAN
Washington, D.C.

ISBN 0-941694-11-9

First Edition, 1964
First *Institute for the Study of Man* Edition, 1983

Copyright © 1983 by Institute for the Study of Man, Inc.
Suite 520, 1629 K Street, N.W.
Washington, D.C. 20006

093651

To the Memory of my Mother,

Mrs. E.C. Bliss

ABOUT THE AUTHOR

It is impressive to realize that the author of *It's Better in America* was himself an immigrant to the United States. Patrick F.H. Mahony was born in England, the son of a courageous British Army officer who was killed in World War I while the future author was still of tender age. This tragic event resulted in the remarriage of Mr. Mahony's bereaved mother, and the removal of the young Mahony to the United States of America, to reside in the homeland of his new step-father. Here he spent a happy childhood in the beautiful town of Santa Barbara, on the Pacific Coast of California.

Although he always retained a fondness for his British and Irish roots, Mr. Mahony saw more clearly than many native-born Americans the dramatic vitality and pervasive charm of his adopted homeland. Choosing the title, *It's Better in America,* a topic on which he frequently lectured before service clubs throughout the nation, Patrick Mahony sat down and wrote an eloquent tribute to the varied romance and beauty of the North American landscape, its history, culture and people. Every page of this book — which won him an Americanism Award from the Daughters of the American Revolution — convincingly reflects the sincerity of his admiration and love for the United States of America.

In *It's Better in America,* Mr. Mahony sought to help readers not only to develop respect, love and pride for the United States, but also to experience something of the deep pleasure which results when an astute sense of observation is combined with a sympathetic feeling for historical atmosphere. All this is done with subtlety and versatility. Those who knew the author will readily recapture the mellow tones of his pleasant, cultured voice while reading, once again, the pages of this entertaining book.

Table of Contents

Prologue

WHAT'S THE MATTER WITH AMERICANS? THEY appear to believe that by going to France, Italy, Germany, Spain, or elsewhere abroad, they will get more per dollar in history and antiquity than in America. They wander over the Old Continent for sights that are inferior to those near at hand in their native land. Some tour Switzerland without having set eyes on the High Sierras or the Olympics. Others go to view the beauties of the Rhine or the Rhone, unaware that river experts have long ago proclaimed the Columbia the most beautiful in the world.

Or you meet those who wax wondrously over French and German caverns yet have not bothered to explore the incredible underground worlds of Carlsbad and Mammoth Caves. By thousands they revel in the delights of rural England, missing the counterpart in our Eastern seaboard. How many world-travelers have missed the unique experience, only available in America, of going to sea by train—across the railway trestle of Utah's Salt Lake? And some even go all the way to New Zealand to astound themselves with a Thermal District dwarfed by the great geysers of Yellowstone.

Why go to Egypt before seeing the wonders of our own antiquity at Mesa Verde Park in Southwest America— where the cliff-cities built by the aboriginal Americans date back further than the first half of our first Millennium? I am amazed at the number of Americans I meet who have never seen that supreme spectacle of Nature, the Grand Canyon of the Colorado. The cry ought to be "See the Grand Canyon—not Naples—and die!" The splendid slogan of that finest of steamship companies, the Cunard Line, that "getting there is half the fun," should work both ways! European tourists should come to us.

For myself I admit to being late in appreciating America. The object of this book is to tell of places, persons, and pieces of Americana which influenced my Americanization. It has no scheme, is not meant to be exhaustive. A book of this kind must be somewhat rambling and a little disconnected because, in the words of Archibald Mac-Leish, America is many lands and many people. I am in hopes I prove that Americans can go abroad without leaving home.

It is not very easy for a man in middle age to admit that he has spent valuable years in pursuit of false delusion. Yet by writing this book in a mood of penance I am admitting just that. For, as many do, I took the privilege of being an American citizen for granted.

A few years ago, during a period of discouragement, I decided to pass a while on the Old Continent, Ireland, and England, where I was born. I had lived the preponderance of my life in the United States but I was beginning to feel "Time's winged chariot" at my back. Mistakenly I thought I might receive more recognition abroad, and I was slowly crossing the bridge that leads to middle age. I was not yet fifty, but thoughts of sixty were already knocking at my heart, rattling in my chest. A deep nostalgia urged me back to the haunts of early years.

Reflecting now, I realize that I was suffering from "Irish

discontent"—in other words that I was mainly discontented with myself. My published books had been written to a large extent to please myself, which is perhaps why they did not reach that wider audience every writer covets.

Just to have been born intelligent is no guarantee that you will always act intelligently. In how many minds does memory march waving the banner of regret? But it was, I know it now, the very contrast I sought that convinced me in the end that my destiny lay in my adoptive land, and I now ask myself how I could ever have considered living permanently anywhere else. American citizenship is an act of will, and I became naturalized because I wanted to be. But to absent myself for very long, as I intended, could have meant losing the privilege—which I nearly did.

First I went to live in Ireland, where I found my English accent no passport into the hearts of her people. With my very Irish name and long residence in America, no one could understand why I had never lost my clipped London pronunciation. My joke failed to amuse the Irish when I said I had lost my Irish brogue at the Battle of the Boyne. It took me about six months to discover that Ireland offered me little except a certain sense of melancholy against which my ancestral compatriots fight by drinking hard.

Incidentally, I nearly purchased a house near Dublin during this period, and I became mildly amused by the chicanery used by local lawyers. None of them inform Americans, as they ought, that if they purchase property in the Emerald Republic they may never be able to get back their invested funds into United States dollars. There are other hazards, too. Within the land-lease of the real estate I was considering, there was a four-hundred-year-old clause which gave the local laird (a member of the feudal English gentry) the right to make me grind his corn each year! When I remonstrated, the laird's lawyer assured me that the right would never be exercised. But he wanted several hundred pounds to sign a quitclaim!

From Ireland I went to the Continent, where I drank draughts from the springs of life—pursuing a rather purposeless life without taking the trouble of testing its truth. Nonetheless, if I admit to being a fool, I must insist that the folly of a Continental man is stiffly self-conscious. He no longer sees in his failings the essential necessity that makes them supportable, nor in the absurdities of society the agreeable folly that makes them diverting. When stupid, he uses his egotism like cocaine to deaden the pain of being a fool!

My own folly has always had a laughing ease with it, helping me to see within myself. I am willing to admit that France is the cradle of civilization, but it rocked me the wrong way! I went to Switzerland where I found the mountains glorious, but the Swiss people so dull one had to rely more and more on their chocolate!

Inevitably I was drawn to my native England, which I had visited during the halcyon days of the 'Thirties. I stayed there nearly a year, finally coming to the conclusion that the "Nationalized" life was not for me. The words of William Butler Yeats came back to me—that the Englishman lies to himself and tells the truth to others; while the Irishman tells the truth to himself and lies to everybody else! As they say in Ireland, you can't put back an uprooted tree.

Because I had become an American citizen I was always treated by officialdom as if I might be an enemy alien. I had committed the unforgivable sin of swearing disal-

legiance to the Royal Family, which hadn't been hard for
me to do. I was, as an Irishman, always rather amused by
the docility with which the English admire their Royalty,
although well aware of the scriptural precept for the idea.

Socially I was treated as if I had never become American. Again and again people whom I met would say to me:
"You're not at all like an American!" which is as insulting
an innuendo were I American or Greek. I found, too, that
some of those Lords and Ladies whom you read about in
the fashionable papers and whom Americans entertain so
lavishly when they come here, would not bother to exchange speech with the average American unless they felt
he might be worth plucking. The few of the so-called "Labor" peers whom I have met, have been cheap snobs.
After accepting a title, they proceed to play off both ends
against the middle.

How well I recall an elegant peeress whom I met at a
party given by an American friend who rather doted on
titles. The peeress was in the decorating business and in
the course of conversation she confided: "I came to meet
this lady, who is a friend of a friend, because I felt she
might be needing a decoration job. Am I right? If not, I
must hurry on to another party." And when I told her that
our hostess already had a decorator engaged for her new
home in London, the peeress left as if a fire had been announced!

All the same, there are many expatriate Americans who
seem to find magic in being thus treated behind their
backs in the whirligig that is London or Paris society. For
some reason they do not sense the anti-Americanism in
both Capitals, which is subterranean. I kept on asking myself why France and England, especially, should resent

American generosity and idealism? I know we were indebted to them for keeping the flame of hope alive in the
War, but does this have to go to the point of genuflection?

I stayed in England nearly a year, finally coming to the
conclusion that the life I had hoped to find—that which
blends the literary and artistic in happy measure—has
completely passed away. I had been led to believe that
writers were granted a modicum of social prestige not
found in America, but I was wrong. Unless a writer man-
ages to make himself famous he is more third class than
second. One of them said to me: "I travel third class because there is no fourth."

To emphasize this, I interviewed an editor about the
possibility of using some articles I had boiling on the pot
I call my mind. He received me in the most bored manner
and showed his hand at once. "I only have to put my head
out of this window and I'll have half a dozen writers lining
up to work for me."

I couldn't resist a thrust. I asked: "Write about what?
Your head?" That ended the interview.

I became more and more disillusioned until one night
an extraordinary thing happened. I had a recurring dream,
or was it a waking vision? I may have been awake when,
gazing into semi-darkness (the room was slightly lit by a
street lamp shining through the window), I saw what I
can only describe as an apparition. A giant figure nearly
reaching the ceiling approached my bed. Although the
face was invisible, I recognized the figure of Uncle Sam. I
felt, rather than I could actually see, the contemplative
frown, almost a scowl. More and more wonderstruck at
his approach, any anxiety I must have felt was quickly
dispelled when the figure spoke. He said in drawling ac-

cent: "Don't you realize that America belongs to you? It is *your* country. Always call it yours."

I wanted to reply, to cry out, to ask questions. As I was raising myself from my pillow, the Spirit lifted its head and a shaft of light fell upon its image. With a shiver of horror I saw that the face was exactly like my own. In a flash I knew the meaning. I had been seeking the will o' the wisp and my contentment rested in remaining a nephew of Uncle Sam. I saw now that unconsciously I had been trying to find my new self within the old shadows of youth.

Of a sudden I yearned to feel the sense of space which one finds in U.S.A., to be back in its huge continent. I felt a sudden nostalgia for the Great Sights of Nature, such as those possessed in our National Park System. After all, Nature's alphabet is the same all over the world and consists of four letters—wood, water, rock, and earth. And within this small alphabet she creates such varied compositions and infinite combinations as no language with an alphabet of twenty-four letters can describe. America contains attractions of mountains, forests, rivers and lakes far surpassing those of Europe, as I shall prove. Nowhere else will you find such sudden glories as to be seen during an Eastern State Autumn, when the Great King holds court with green and gold arising from woods, grass, and cornfields.

In this moment of insight and outlook, I was able to see that my main trouble was that I had not been on right terms with the workaday world and thus could not claim from it comfort or respect. From now on I must adjust and come into rank with the rest of the world—the rear rank, maybe—but with an untiring urge to march in step. From now on, I must adapt to what I found wrong with

America and come to better terms with its human environment.

So it was farewell to the cursed years of homeless wandering. I may say, in passing, that I envy those so fortunate as to have been born in America for they never feel the pull exerted by a mother land elsewhere. There are those who believe that we are born again and again—rising and sinking in various existences according to how we behave. If this is true—and I suspect that it be—I will try to earn the right Karma to be born next time a native American.

In every page the spirit of rediscovery has seized me, and it has been forcibly borne in upon me that the important things of life are those we re-discover. Slight misconceptions are inevitable when writing on so vast a subject. I realize only too well that in one sense a country can only be fully understood by its own children. A motherland is like a jealous woman whispering her closest secrets to her own.

In another sense, however, the adoptive citizen has added powers of observation for certain peculiar features which escape the born American. This is proved by the fact that some of the best-known Americanists are men such as Sir Denis Brogan, whom I suspect is Anglo-Irish and certainly was born outside America. In my case, any misconceptions are, I believe, those subtleties on which any non-native American might stumble.

Mindful of what the great humorist Josh Billings once said: "There's something worse than ignorance and that's knowing what ain't so," I have read numberless books on the United States for accuracy. And I am, of course, indebted in many ways to many people, especially the staff of that wonderful institution called the New York Public Library, where the books on my subjects have kindled many a thought of my own. I must thank Hermann Hagedorn for urging me to set a higher standard for myself than I originally intended. Mrs. Clifford Wilson Cueman of Fredericksburg, Virginia, has given me valuable editorial assistance, especially on the piece I have included on her native State, which I was better able to appreciate as seen through the lens of her love for it. I must also thank Storm Publishers, Inc. for their gracious permission to use short excerpts from my books *You can find a way* and *Out of the silence*.

As I have said, the subjects treated emerge from the jungle of my mind as completing me an American. I realize now that the actual process was not sufficient, that Americanization must be experienced so that it may ripen, perhaps long after the oath has been taken. It has been borne in upon me again and again that the most permanent force in America is change and how hard it is to keep abreast of the teeming problems caused by change. It is also difficult not to feel an overmastering importance of these years which I have passed abroad, when so much has been in transition—that in one way and another they may point to solve some of our pressing problems. Viewed from the perspective of distance, I have been extremely conscious that world leadership for America carries with it the risk of failure, which must be unthinkable. So here is one small but positive voice from the grandstand.

It's Better in America

ONE MUST DISTINGUISH BETWEEN AMERICA'S spirit, which is to be found within the pages of recorded speeches and letters of our great leaders since the earliest days, and what can only be termed the nation's Psyche or Soul. This is made up of the forces formed from the collective inner consciousness that becomes transmuted into a national psychology. They in turn form the environment in which we house or reason and are the basis of our national life. By better comprehending them we may aid in the self-conscious creation of our own role in our country's history.

Self-knowledge through history is everyone's duty as a good citizen, the discharge of which is essential for the national health. Long ago that great Greek scholar, Thucydides, noted its importance. His profound inquiry into history revealed to him the powers of the past, especially the perpetuation of past errors in the present. "Whoever shall wish," says he, in that cogent style every reader admires, "to learn the truth about past events and to deduce therefrom the course which events in all human possibility may follow—let them adjudge my History usefully and I shall be satisfied . . ."

We should try to grasp the fact that the historic past is a living past and by its study we can make new steps forward in self-discipline. For if one thinks about it, the historic process of human development interpenetrates life and logic in such a way that our national philosophy is continually being submitted to verification. By carefully acquainting ourselves with the historic past, we become more firmly a part of American life and function more fully as an integral part of it. If more people would take a refresher course in it, our country would be spiritually reborn and restrengthened. They would find that History is a torch which can light the future as well as the past.

Nations have their souls to guard, just as individuals do. If ever you wish to feel the throbbing of the American soul, go to Independence Hall in Philadelphia. Under that roof you sense symbolically the crucible in which this Nation was alchemized like gold. There you may see those relics, insignificant in themselves but representing the mysticism of courage when the future was in doubt— all piously guarded by the portraits of the men who helped to make America. If you listen with your third ear, you may hear that great symphony, the leitmotif which is always reheard during periods of heroic struggle.

Under a constitutional government such as ours the national soul will depend more and more on the moral qualities of the many, rather than the few. Obviously the same qualities which determine the soul of the individual, which is you, also determine the soul of the nation. It is trite to say that every good American must feel a personal responsibility for the governmental policies at home and abroad and for a satisfactory administration of public affairs. I am touching on that treasury of experience which, if rich, can issue forth in social progress and improvement—if misused, in delusions, and failure.

Think of the most glorious chapters of American history. They are those recording the sufferings and trials through which the soul of the nation was founded and developed. It is altogether probable that the Revolutionary War represents to America what the Elizabethan Age is to England—the epoch on which Patriotism fixes its eye for its image. In a psychic sense the great dead continue to live on in a nation and control it unknown to itself (and I do not mean Spiritualism). Great souls, from George Washington to Lincoln, still elevate and uphold America, shedding over it the glory of their supreme bequests. No country need ever feel lost that feels itself guarded by such noble witnesses.

Within America's soul is a yearning to serve humanity. That is why she always tries to be the yeast that leavens the world. But here lies the rub: Patriotism and humanity are apt to be antagonistic. The latter is not a distinct idea and the two sources cannot always be in agreement. Humanity, as the sum total of all mankind, tells us little. Our sense of humanity is based on a demand for justice to all men. America will always be an instrument for serving humanity in this sense.

Yet no informed person regards perfection in his own land or abroad to be attainable or even necessary. In spite of America's great idealism her goal has never been one of flawless excellence. Perfect spiritual harmony in people is exceedingly rare and even then is reached only in brief periods of exaltation or self-surrender. It can also make them bovine!

Were anyone to ask me what I feel is America's greatest achievement, I think I would find it hard to decide between religious equality or the peaceful coexistence of so many varying nationalities, who would perhaps be warring continually on the borders of their own lands. Thus America has demonstrated the unity of mankind—a forecast of World Federation which *must* come sooner or later. Ultimately the world will have to become a group of United Republics, and only then will the United Nations be truly effective.

The main obstacle of bringing about One World is in winning over to us those nations not in sympathy with our ideals. We must make the best of great inconveniences and try to keep preaching that man as a whole is an exchanging animal—the only exchanging animal! Individuals buy, but nations must exchange. Politically I am not really of any party and the names on a bottle matter little to me, provided the contents are good. All political parties should impress on themselves a sense of their shortcomings and aim at gathering knowledge continually which will be useful in their regulation of service.

Or if someone were to ask me what I like best about America, I believe I would have to say it is that intangible factor which challenges my spirit—that something which is indefinable because it is a little conglomerate and even chaotic. It keeps on telling me that I must hurry up and get things done. It tells me that defeat is never total and more chances than one may come my way in anything I may essay. It is a factor that stimulates.

And if I were requested to define the American spirit in a few words I would be unable. I would have to refer to the pages of books and diaries by our great leaders—Jefferson, Washington, Lincoln, John Quincy Adams, and others lesser known—some of them cruelly neglected.

I would add that it is anything but a young spirit, and I am heartily tired of hearing foreigners say that America is a young country. It never was. As a State it is young, of course, but the splendid power of our political and moral ideas is deeply rooted in the last thousand years or so. These sprang from the minds of the Founding Pilgrim Fathers, the oldest souls on earth. Is it without significance that Uncle Sam is portrayed as an elderly man? Or that Ponce de Leon came here to find the Fountain of Youth and failed?

Only a race of old souls would cry, "Too old at thirty-five!" Isn't it obvious that those who insist that the voice of age is the voice of wisdom are the immature? It is only an old people who insist, as does America, that imagination and creativity die (to some extent at least) when youth dies. Youth is now at the helm and it is going to stay there.

Anyone who takes the trouble to examine carefully the Constitution of the United States can see that it was the product of very mature minds, which had inherited the Puritan tradition profoundly. This formative force, an urgent creative urge, explored the full complement of human qualities. It is directly from these old souls that America has inherited the sense of duty as being a mystical rite on which the claim of humanity forces attention.

It was through the Puritan ideas that there arose the recognition of humanity as a perennial power, inspired by a persistent aim of working out on our planet a scheme for universal good—to serve humanity within attainable limits. The idea of doing one's duty was enunciated here long before Lord Nelson's order at Trafalgar. It is the type of unique function, voluntarily discharged, guaranteed to every American to be free to do it—and within reasonable limits to be assisted by his fellow citizens.

Of course, the old proud Colonial stock has been diluted
by the successive waves of immigration. But that is
another secret source of our power. America has attained
her higher destiny from these hordes that have been
brought to her shores. She has gained in proportion to
what she has lost of the old stock by this dilution. A list
of great names of Americans born abroad would fill another book, beginning with Alexander Hamilton, who
emigrated from the Leeward Isles. This does not alter the
fact that we have inherited the Puritan tradition profoundly and that it blends well with the modern spirit.

A glance at the very early days in New England will
prove that America began with a certain amount of hu-
manitarian socialism. In Massachusetts no sphere of life
was free from State regulation, and this was often directed
against monopolies. In 1639 we find the Rev. Mr. Cotton
saying (for the State, in those Theocratic days) words in
denunciation of numerous false principles, among which
were "that a man may buy as cheap as he can and sell as
dear . . ." Is it any wonder that sooner or later free
competition became an avowed American principle?

Since the Founding Fathers arrived, since the break-
down of Aristocracy, which freed men from Paternalism
and made Democracy possible, America has challenged
danger and defied the Fates for her ideas. Optimism has
always been so contagious that the worst crisis has bred
the longest patience and the hardest toil the finest efforts.
Great misfortunes have occurred, but these have developed the nation as it does the lives of the best men.

What has always been attractive for me in the native
born American is a certain temperamental trait of readi-

ness and willingness to learn. There is a mental quickness, what the French call the "coup d'oeil," plus a desire to adopt and adapt methods used abroad in almost every line of achievement. He realizes the premium placed on imagination and creativity. The immigrant, placed suddenly on the broad lap of Uncle Sam, soon falls under this spell and develops a new environment of happiness.

For that reason I have always wished that the Blue Bird had been chosen for the American symbol instead of the Eagle, which is a rare predatory bird these days and its meaning can be misinterpreted by ill-disposed people. Moreover, it was long ago appropriated by certain foreign monarchies. In their favor, Blue Birds are found all over U.S.A. and represent happiness. I also wish that Uncle Sam could be known as Brother Sam, because America has become the half-brother of the Western World!

The American soul has undergone several periods of self-discovery and will doubtless go through many more. In fact, our temper as a people has been the outcome of much vaster influences than our critics have been willing to recognize. The Constitution, which suits the American soul so well, was the result of endless argument and compromise. Like all great ideas, it was rooted in a blend of thought and dreams, and it is essential that we go on dreaming these dreams or the future may one day belong to those who do.

As long as we delight in ideals that touch the heart as well as the head, we will solve our problems and also help our friends solve theirs. Our greatest hope lies in the demonstrated proof that American ideas are at once abstract, powerful and startling. They always have been and always will. Even the least influential amongst us can see that thoughts are positive and constructive—for it is mass thoughts that really rule the world.

We *will* solve our problems because we are a land of faith, and faith is mainly a point of view, the way you regard the ultimate things. We do not have to be believers in the sense of being devout and pious, nor in the meaning of renunciation. The faith I mean is a quality of thought, and the only man who does not have it does no thinking.

In a more personal sense, Americans with a soul have faith in themselves like that expressed by the winning oarsmen of Virgil's Aeneid: "We can because we think we can." Our greatest desideratum, however, is to find unity amid diversity in whatever attainable measure is possible. It can only be done by the same faith that spring is born of winter—sure in its belief that the destiny of humanity is an integral part of creation.

Going Abroad in California   I. 2

THERE ARE TWO THEORIES AS TO HOW CALIfornia got its name, one being that Cortez christened her first in Latin, *Calida Formax* (Hot Furnace). But I think the other the more likely—that the early discoverers called her Calafia, which became deflected into its present form. Queen Calafia is said to have ruled over a mythical island, peopled by dusky Amazons, who bestrode great beasts and wore trappings of gold.

These explorers at first mistook their discovery for an island because it looked to them separated from the mainland by dint of its long gulf. If we think about it, the name they chose was very suitable because the beginning of California is wrapped in mystery with legends of Aztec origin. When one turns the mind beyond the Spanish rule, it flounders in the void. No one knows what strange races came and went in those canoe-going days.

The State only became a member of the Union in 1850, and her great popularity for a healthful climate is much more recent. This dates from the time that doctors discovered that sunlight is therapeutic, bactericidal, and analgesic. They were very late in rediscovering what the Greeks always knew—or at least discovered over two thousand years ago—that sunlight raises the fight in the blood to combat disease.

Doctors began about 1880 sending people to California, which they said contained one of the best drugs in the entire Pharmacopoeia, now called Vitamin D. They had forgotten, or overlooked, that the Greeks made Apollo not only god of Light and the Arts, but also god of Medicine—which was their particular way of saying that the sun is bactericidal and analgesic!

I sometimes think that the publicity departments of the State of California are in need of overhauling. Most people think of her as being a broad strip of land and series of valleys between the mountains and the Pacific. Unfortunately, the publicity is usually designed to increase the number of real estate investors, and they never tell of fascinating parts of the State not already famous.

So it happens that many tourists who go to the West Coast
see only the West Coast, which no one would deny is one
long stretch of delight, fretted by a sapphire sea. Here, in
fact, man has dealt very royally with Nature, and there is
very little left to be done—except buy your home.

But there are wondrous parts of California not fre-
quented by tourists. Over the mountains in the North and
South, spring usually opens a month later than below. It
is a land more untouched than that of the Coast—a land
of rivers, of ancient boulders perched on tottering crags,
of wayside inns, of wonderful roads winding through
booming gorges, of olive orchards and cool Pueblo
churches, where lie the bones of many a forgotten prelate.

There are hamlets that nestle in the wrinkle of the hills,
hovered over by a great silence save for the everpresent
sound of insects and birds. It is hard to say which time is
the more beautiful—in May, just after the chill winds of
winter, or when the Autumnal rains are finished. It is a
pastoral haven wherever you go. The hills and valleys
seemingly roll together and are interspersed with farms
and vineyards. When all is burgeoning down below,
everything is in small bud up here.

My own first entrance into the Sunset State was by ship,
through the Golden Gate. Those fortunate as I was to see
a Golden Sunset illuminating the low-lying hills that surround the shore, will feel that the name is all the more
appropriate. The Gate is five miles long by one mile wide
and the Bay is about sixty miles in length—so enormous
that it is capable of holding all the Navies of the world.

Rumor has it that Sir Francis Drake beached his *Golden
Hind* somewhere on these shores. Preserved in the Library
of the University of California, at Berkeley, is a large

brass plate found washed up on the shores of this Bay in 1954. It was corroded and showed evidence of having been in the sea a very long time. On the plate is a hole the size of an Elizabethan sixpence, such as might have been used as a substitute for the Royal Seal. Not without difficulty you may read the inscription, which has been alternately branded genuine and a forgery:

"Bee it knowne vnto all men by these presents June 17, 1579:

"By Grace of God in name of Herr Maiestie Qveen Elizabeth of England and Herr successors forever I take possession of this Kingdom whose king and people freely recognize their right and title in the whole land vnto Herr Maiestie's keeping now named by me and to bee knowne vnto all men as Nova Albion. Francis Drake."

It is known that Drake penetrated into the Northwest, but this proof that he may have actually set foot near the City of San Francisco pleases anyone with a sense of history. Miles of charming drives border the water and you may speculate just where the great adventurer landed, if he ever did. You may be sure of seeing hundreds of seals cavorting on the rocks, also of hearing their barking amid the roaring of the breakers.

The City of San Francisco, named after St. Francis of Assisi, is often called the "Paris of the West." And its shops and restaurants have a Parisian air, giving the city a vivacious personality unique among other American cities. Fruit and flower stalls in the streets present splashes of color, and the presence of Chinese and Japanese shops in their respective districts add a flavor of the East.

On the famous Nob Hill there are a number of homes that once belonged to the Bonanza Kings. Like Rome, San Francisco is built on many hills, some of which are much steeper than in the Eternal City. Unlike Rome the city stands on the East shore of the North end of a long peninsula. It is situated geographically rather like New York City—at the base of sandy hills on a slope that extends into the Bay. Anchored in the middle is the forbidding island of Alcatraz.

From San Francisco you can radiate further North into the Bret Harte country. To recreate this land, which the great writer made famous, one needs only to turn to his books, which thinly varnish the exciting truth of the good old days—when these ghost towns were full of saloons and brothels, enlivened by glamorous ladies and brutal murders. Once so boisterously alive with seekers after gold and silver, they are now no more than museums of the past. All the same, there is deeply etched the romantic quality which the genius of Bret Harte caught.

In Napa Valley, the heart of the wine industry, one motors through miles of sweet-smelling vineyards, reminiscent of Spain or Italy. There is something inexpressibly appealing as the eye ranges over these hundreds of acres presided over by distant mountains. I believe that I have never seen in Southern Europe a sight comparable to the melting beauty of these scenes at evening. It offers the peace that passes all understanding.

Here and there you have a touch of French architecture, for some of the wineries are in good imitation of the Touraine Chateaux. And Californian wines equal the comparison of the French, matching the test very well. The grapes produce a small degree of stronger fermentation due to the greater carbohydrates, giving the wine a slightly higher alcoholic content.

At St. Helena there is a remarkable petrified forest, well worth a visit. At the foot of the titular mountain is one of many sulphur springs, the waters of which rival the average European Spa in helping rheumatic woes. Passing over Mount St. Helena, you are on your way to the Lake Country, a region immortalized by Robert Louis Stevenson in his *Silverado Squatters*. For the student of aboriginal lore there is much to see en route, in the form of primitive art work done by the Indians.

For the poet, there are scenes surpassing the dells and dales which made Wordsworth and Coleridge lyrical in England. We see, softened by the altitudinous atmosphere, dream-like fascades of rock formations, some of unique outline. They make one feel that a good mythologist is needed to create tales about them, as they do in Ireland about some less striking.

Those who feel like relaxing taut nerves should pay a visit to the Giant Sequoia trees in the High Sierras. The Sequoia National Park is named after an illiterate Indian Chief named Sequoyah. This remarkable Cherokee, born in Tennessee, has confounded scholars with his creation of an alphabet for the language of his tribe. From its phonetics he invented ideographic symbols that broke down the units and sounds, reducing them to eighty-five in all. Thus, in 1809, his people were able for the first time to communicate with the outer world. Chief Sequoyah is considered to be for his people what Cadmus was to the Phoenicians, because he freed them from ignorance by the invention of a written language. Overnight he made the great Cherokee Nation literate, but the work it took cost him his health and he died soon afterwards.

So it is fitting that these marvels of tree growth should be named after a man who did such wonders for his race. At Sequoia National Park you step into a world of silence and pine-scented air, a solitude forgotten by bustling time. Who can stand unmoved amid these majestic tree shapes seen in all their primal simplicity and splendor? You cannot see their like anywhere else in the world, not even in Syria where the Cedars of Lebanon were once a great sight. Incidentally, these Sequoias are the same genus (though perhaps not the same species) as the Lebanese. Both were mature when the Egyptians were building their Pyramids!

There are miles and miles of them in the Park, some even three hundred feet high and from eighty to ninety feet in circumference. They make the Forest of Fontainebleau seem very tame by comparison. A brisk trade is done in exporting cones for transplantation. These are about the size of a hen's egg and they take three years from the budding stage to the ripening.

It is a spiritualizing experience to pass a few days in the shade of these overwhelming trees. Some distance away is the Mariposa Grove, discovered by a one-time Sheriff of Mariposa County, hence the name. It consists of ten groves scattered along the west front of the Sierra Range for nearly two hundred miles. These are closely related to the Sequoias at the Park and many are named after famous men. There is one called George Washington, which is ninety feet tall, and two others (not so tall!) in memory of Longfellow and Whittier. I myself wrote a poem when I visited the Grove, beginning: "I think that I shall never see a billboard lovely as a tree!" (apologies to Joyce Kilmer, of course). Happily, there are no billboards in this area.

Excursions to Sequoia National Park are usually combined with a trip to Yosemite Valley, written about so extensively I shall not add more than one speck to the sea of ink already spilled upon its glories. A river flows musically through this wondrous wooded ravine, which is of such savage and entrancing beauty—hemmed in by masses of gigantic basaltic rock. I have been through the noted European gorges, when en route to the South of France, such as those in the Tarne Valley (I have also seen the Cheddar Gorge in England), but none is in any wise so striking as the verticality of rock formation that one sees all around one in Yosemite.

Numerous crags scatter the wooded summits with strange and imposing forms. Some dart into the heavens, as if they were astronaut rockets ready for shooting into space. Others are arranged in battle formation; still others raise lonely, phantom-like peaks in vast isolated spaces. Dawn and evening cast just the right light on them, suggesting that they must have been left there by some giant, absent-minded god! Night puts them to sleep by extinguishing them altogether.

As one contemplates a journey south, the land of eternal summer beckons. It should never be forgotten that it was climate and not gold that made California the brightest in our Constellation of States. Climate brought the citrus industry; it also attracted the film tycoons to form their empire and set up a world Capital there. Oddly enough, the health-giving value of the State was first publicized by

Charles Nordoff, the father of the author of *The Mutiny on the Bounty*.

His book burned like so much dry grass through the reading public of America in 1870, starting a trek of health-seekers to the "Sunkissed State," as Nordoff called it. California was grateful to him and named a town after him, which was rechristened Ojai later on. His only memory now reposes there in the local school, which bears his name.

So it is to the Southland that we should make our way and, as in the *Côte d'Azur*, there are two routes to consider. If you go inland, you may see the lovely enclosed valley where dozes the little town of San Juan Bautista, now a museum. This was once the headquarters of General Castro who marched from it to the capitulation of Cahuengha—then a Spanish stronghold a long way South and now a famous pass through which the Hollywood Freeway winds. San Juan Bautista's Mission is a gem-like sample and in good repair.

Scenically the route by the Coast is far superior, being unequalled by any similar stretch in the State. You leave San Francisco, taking a last look to the North, where at evening the hills of Marin County are often seen in purple shadows, clustering around the base of Mount Tamalpais. Passing through Burlingame, don't fail to see some of the show estates and note how the homes and gardens spread themselves in the Spanish and Italian manner. Some of these are true masterpieces, and to their owners such paradises that they are said not to notice the change when they reach the real Heaven!

Palo Alto is symbolized by the lone Redwood pine that gave the name to this celebrated University town. Stanford's palm-lined campus stresses the Spanish style, with Byzantine touches. Not generally known is that this great University owes its being to the ghost of a young man, the son of the one-time Governor of California, who was Leland Stanford. The death of his son at an untimely age led the Governor and his wife to attend Spiritualistic séances in which the spirit of their dead son seemingly materialized. It urged his wealthy father to endow an institution for the purpose of higher learning, which he did. In the founding covenant it was laid down that the University was to be non-sectarian—except for an elective course in the Immortality of the Soul.

A stop at Monterey is most rewarding, for here is the finest array of Spanish adobes in the State, with their pottery roofs and whitewashed walls set in charming gardens blooming with roses, fuchias and geraniums. Here Vizcaino landed to take possession in the name of the King of Spain, calling it Monterey, which means Mountain Kingdom. It was here, too, that Father Junipero Serra landed to found his second Mission for Upper California.

From the garden of his Church you get a lovely view of the curving Coast, shimmering in sand and surf. Landwards there is a wide scanning of hills covered with pines and oaks—all forming the immense amphitheater which contains the old town. The Stars and Stripes were abortively raised here in 1846, then re-raised in 1848.

Among the many adobes, Colton House has been carefully reconstructed and is reminiscent of a stately Virginian mansion. Another, Larkin House, seems laden with ghosts. Its owner, James Larkin (of Irish descent), left behind a diary, a published account of the good old gracious days, now gone forever.

Therein he tells of colorful events, of weddings enhanced by Spanish girls dancing the Fandango, their cava-
liers partnering them to music from guitar and mandolin.
There are entries about long rides over sheep ranges, of
bull and bear fights, and it would seem that Mr. Larkin
and his friends passed their lives in energetic idling, taking
time off for industrious observation!

According to the diary, no dearth of gossip existed.
Scandal was transmitted by what he calls the "Monterey
Washerwoman Express," by which news travelled faster
than the fastest Indian runner! Revenants linger in the
patios of the adobes, and you may repeople the scene with
the vanished tenants siestering at noon in the shadow of
waving palms, and listening to the songs of summer. A
strong feeling of romance still hovers over this dear old
Californian town which will entice you back to Monterey.
Robert Louis Stevenson's house is now a museum, but his
love for this part of California is better appreciated within
the covers of a book he wrote on it.

Carmel-by-the-Sea provides breathtaking seascapes. No
wonder that film companies choose it when they need
scenery for the wilder stretches of English coastlines.
Dense woods embosom the village, making its winter
climate extraordinarily mild for Northern California.
Further South is Big Sur which they say is crawling with
artists and writers, all enchanted with its scenic beauty.
Keep hugging the Coast instead of taking the adopted
highway. On this road, called locally "the Corkscrew,"
there is truly no destination—only pauses to stop and
admire the long stretches of coast with its concavity of
curve defined by sheltering headlands.

You wind along a series of hairpin turns, the ocean

waves curling and breaking with infinite variety below the elevation of the cliffs, giving the finishing touch to this scenery of poetic appeal. Soon you join the main highway which takes you in rapid succession through towns with such romantic pasts as Salinas and Paso Robles, where you may care to reflect that the renowned Polish pianist, Paderewski, once lived and regained his lost health by taking the local mud baths.

The Santa Clara Valley is one stretch of delight if seen beneath the vault of a Californian azure. Nature has indeed been prodigal to this district. Everywhere are classical scenes of citrus groves against a background of mountains. There are groves and groves of them, together with Walnut plantations, usually lined with Oriental-looking Palms. Those mountains in the distance house all the minerals known to Geology. The further South you get, the more you will find all the fruits and flowers known to mankind.

In California you have all the climates known to man, but the season of any Southern Californian valley begins when you arrive. In vain you look for winter at Christmas, and instead you see the contrast of white orange blossoms against a distant backdrop of snowcapped peaks. Wherever you go, the countryside will be a carnival of flowers —flaunting their bright smiles. On the hillsides Yucca and Century plants, which the Indians used for food and clothing, grow side by side of pines and spruce trees. Here are banana, coconut, pomegranate, cork and rubber trees in pleasing variety.

Soon the Santa Barbara Channel Islands heave to view. Time was when freebooters and pirates sang and shouted there in their cups, waiting to prey on galleons carrying

precious cargo from the Orient. Santa Cruz Island contains a former smuggler's cove used for over a hundred
years up until Prohibition days, also a grave said to be
that of Juan Cabrillo. Anacapa lies leeward, to be admired
through binoculars for its steep cliffs covered by a lush
weed growth. Another isle, named Santa Rosa, is now used
for cattle-ranching.

The town of Santa Barbara (the American Mentone)
was called by Barnum "a place where old people can go to
die, but fail in their undertaking!" It was named after
Saint Barbara, who was martyred in the Third Century.
The town owns the Queen of all Missions, which was consecrated on her festival day in 1782. It is an impressively
beautiful edifice and in the old days was surrounded by
numerous Indian huts, presided over by Chief Yanonali—
a docile fellow who let the Spanish invaders in without let
or hindrance. He supervised his tribe in building the Mission. In his day, herds of sheep decorated the Mission's
landscape, now covered with comfortable villas.

The first English-speaking visitor to arrive in Santa
Barbara was actually an English pirate whom the Spanish
called *José el Ingles*, but whose real name was plain John
Chapman. He was enslaved by them for a time, but later
he managed to make himself useful, and was freed. Later
on he married the most beautiful and richest woman in
town and lived happily ever afterward. Many another
has won the heart of the richest (if not the most beautiful)
Santa Barbara woman up until very recent times!

Each year, at the time of full moon, there is a lively
Fiesta, also Maria Margelli's *Battle of the Flowers*. Gardens in Santa Barbara are considered finer than any other

town of its size in America, not least of which is that of the Old Mission—where troubles seem aloof to the world.

By far the most spectacular is *Lotusland,* created by Madame Ganna Walska, the Polish singer, which is considered a work of art. Here, amid Cacti arranged in familiar habitat and a sizable lotus pond, there is the feeling that the veil between this and the true paradise is inordinately thin.

Situated poetically between the mountains and the sea, Santa Barbara can best be appreciated from an eminence. Here are some impressions I received watching the spectacle some years ago on a summer day, until evening:

The sun rises peacefully, bathing the rich verdure in an opalescent hue. White tufts of mist, dispersing gradually, hang over the Pacific like fragments of a torn veil. The faint pale lilac of the horizon silhouettes the distant islands, which are delicate and clear.

The whole town basks in the feast of light. Everything is green and many-toned, and the architecture has a hard time competing; at best it can only submit. It all seems cosily shut in by a huge fringe of eucalyptus trees, which tread their way over a rising hill. The Old Mission's rose-colored dome emits the sound of a bell, vigorously rung.

Noonday shines with languishing warmth amid the azure vase of earth and sky. A soft blush suffuses the horizon, turning the sea into a translucent blue, streaked with purple. The distant shore threads its way far below following the indented beaches, with surf white as milk. The entire curving coastline is drenched in the brightness, as it wavers away into the shimmering distances. All is quiet,

save for the sound of birds, the rustling of leaves, and the
hum of insects.

And now evening approaches. The mountain peaks
stand out, dark, sombre, and terrifying. All the prom-
ontories submerge into silhouettes. The coast seems ready
to shrink into itself, and the more distant headlands become a mere succession of ghosts.

Evening stars light up the blue dome as the Milky Way
traces its lingering path. From the sky's center the moon
looks out expectantly, casting enormous shadows. The sea,
phantom-like and dead-still, softly reflects the fading
scene. Night has fallen!

The best photographs of scenery have a terrible defect
because they have not been processed by thought. I hope
I have managed to convey the mood of the soul which
Santa Barbara is capable of evoking. It is equal in every
way to the natural scenery of Capri, about which most
writers become lyrical.

The distance to Los Angeles is a matter of about one
hundred miles. En route one should not miss an idyllic
small Mission at Ventura, with a diminutive garden that
seemingly walks right inside. The old Church seems a
trifle lost in these times, tucked away among modern
buildings. Once it stood as the Spanish padres meant, with
unobstructed views of mountains and sea.

Again you have a choice of two routes south. The coast
road to Santa Monica is very *en Corniche,* offering such
seascapes as one sees when going from Nice to Mentone.
By the alternative route the scenery is also *en grand* in a
way that might inspire a composer to write some awe-in-

spiring music. The famous Conejo Grade offers sweeps of picturesque scenes which take one back to Granada.

Perhaps the most interesting aspect in touring California for a foreign visitor is the strong hold the Spanish nomenclature has retained on the topography. Note the many musical and sonorous names which you come across all over the State. These soft-sounding Spanish names are in pleasing contrast to those harsher used elsewhere in America, often derived from Indian phonetics. This is because the Spanish discoverers named rivers, hills, and villages for favorite saints. Such a charming use of the abstract has rendered a service which time will never banish.

Wherever you go, you feel a wonderful sense of the pioneer vitality and individuality of the Spanish race, stamped indelibly on land and map. Along these sunny foothills, these sequestered valleys, the gentle missionaries planted vines and fig trees. These goodhearted monks anticipated the treasured industry later created by American pioneers by cultivating citrus on the Californian wastes, now the supplier of a world market.

There is a charming rumor that these fathers were responsible for the acres of wild flower phenomena that make certain parts a blaze of color each spring. It is said that they strewed poppy and mustard seeds behind their journeying from Mission to Mission in order to act as a guide for the devout when travelling from one to another. The carpets of these flowers are certainly thickest along these old routes.

A hasty glance at the map will show how the configuration of California obeys the Andine structure of the great Pacific littoral. There are the same paralleling mountain ranges and longitudinal valleys that are found in Peru, Mexico, and Chile, the same corresponding climates and vegetation.

The city of Los Angeles has been described as "a series of suburbs in search of a city," and for me the greatest pleasure has been to be able to radiate away from it in so many interesting directions. Beverly Hills oozes opulence but not many people know that at one time the district cast up one of the greatest Paleontological finds the world has ever known. Certainly it was a greater drama than any dreamt up by the Hollywood fiction-factory.

In the early days of Los Angeles the La Brea Pits, an ugly bog of tar (named after a lake of that name in Trinidad which Sir Walter Raleigh once used for caulking the seams of a wrecked vessel), was used by residents for roofing their houses. The Pits are situated just off Wilshire Boulevard and are located in what is now known as Hancock Park, near Beverly Hills.

One day an enterprising student in Paleontology did some excavation. Out of the bubbling pitch, he fished such Prehistoric mammals as sabre-toothed tigers, camels, horses, giant wolves and a few great ground sloths. All these weird Prehistoric animals had been trapped in the sinking bog about twenty-five million years ago! Good specimens are now to be seen at the Los Angeles Natural History Museum, but the La Brea Pits remains an attraction little known even to local residents.

If you wish the continual sense of being abroad (which is certainly not fostered in Los Angeles), the nearest side-trip is to Palos Verdes Estates—only a matter of twenty miles from downtown. There you may take drives which match any in Capri or Sorrento, even in their gayest moods. The entrance to the Estates, once privately owned but now a residential settlement, is guarded by one of the thickest groves of Eucalyptus I have ever seen. All tints— from the olive to the Chaparral or the somber darkness of the evergreen make it a unique plantation. This hardy species of tree gives off the air of being native instead of looking Australian, from whence it comes.

Take any of the Cliff drives for sights of bold headlands with the sea drenching them in rhythmic waves. Long stretches of rolling hills on which are perched pretty bungalows mindful of the Italian Riviera, where the scenery also culminates in cliffs. Seen from the verge of these precipices, the sea stands incredibly high—a majestic immensity as you might feel from the ruined Palace of Tiberius at Capri.

Not far away the steamers ply to and from Santa Catalina Island, which lies twenty-five miles from the shore. To me Avalon Harbor is a replica of Villefranche in Southern France, and the island itself comparable to Porquorelle, off the Coast of Hyères. The winters at Santa Catalina are milder, proven by the outdoor aviary in which tropical birds flourish, and inhabitants think nothing of catching tuna in the off-shore waters weighing two hundred pounds—or even a swordfish riding three hundred and fifty!

Further out to sea you catch a glimpse of San Clemente Island, about thirty miles South. No one would link this remote spot of U.S.A. with the Vatican in Rome, yet there is one. Some treasured relics from this island are to be seen in the Holy Museum which call to mind a sad story of bygone days.

In 1835 the Government of California decided to re-

move from the Island a number of Indians, for their own
safety. They had been the only inhabitants for many
years, eking out a meagre living and often cut-off from
the mainland in winter. Accordingly the colony was
rounded up, but for some reason a young Squaw was
left behind. Swells were over fifty feet and another land-
ing could not be made at the time. A few days later a boat
went to bring her to join her tribe, but after diligent
searching of the Island, she could not be found. Mysteriously she had vanished, and it was thought that she
might have fallen off one of the cliffs into the sea—and she
became forgotten.

However, she had not died and had, in fact, purposely
remained behind because she mistrusted the civilized
world. For twenty years she lived alone on St. Clemente
Island, with only the sound of birds and the waves of the
sea for company. She lived on fish caught with the few
utensils left behind. As her clothes wore out, she made
herself some with birdskins.

Then one day in 1853 a passing ship sighted her. The
skipper beached his boat and brought the Squaw to San
Pedro, where her fears of civilization proved to be well
founded. The noise and confusion of it all acted so ad-
versely on her nervous system that she died within a few
days. Priests who attended her last moment decided to
send her birdskin dress and sandals to the Vatican Museum, where they now repose.

Anyone feeling like a touch of England should go to
the Huntingdon Museum at San Marino near Pasadena,
which is packed with superb examples of work by Reyn-
olds, Romney, Constable and Gainsborough. They are
sumptuously housed in rooms designed and furnished in

the style of their own period. You see the *Blue Boy* and *Pinkie* on either side of a Georgian fireplace in the drawing room, as if they were "to the Manor" hung—but both gaze unseeingly onto the sub-tropical San Gabriel Valley outside.

At Santiago, in Orange County, Henryk Sienkiewicz lived for a while in 1880. The famous Polish author of *Quo Vadis* was a man of original ideas, one of which embraced his own particular form of Utopian communism. Here he founded a colony, with a score of other Poles, where they could live in a state of brotherly love.

Among the members of the Colony was a beautiful Polish Countess who later became one of America's leading actresses—the divine Madame Modjeska. The Colony didn't last long and Sienkiewicz returned to Poland, but when Madame Modjeska gave up her stage career, she retired there and the place where she settled became known as Modjeska, which is a thriving community and now thoroughly Americanized.

Continuing South the town of San Bernardino, named after the early Franciscan Saint of Siena, is the gateway to several Mountain resorts. Passing through Riverside, where the Inn combines modern comfort with the charm of bygone days, take note of the hundreds of orange groves which are bent with the weight of a very special fruit that has a romantic history of travel. The Bahia orange, sometimes called the Washington Navel, came from Brazil, and in all orange culture there is no such amazing story.

Now exported from California to all parts of the world, this orange was originally brought from Asia to Spain where it throve. Then, in the Sixteenth Century, Portu-

guese navigators took cuttings of it to Brazil and it soon
burgeoned there in groves. Many years later a Mr. Judson,
then United States Consul to Rio, took a young tree to his
ranch in Riverside, upon his retirement from the Foreign
Service. Thus the Bahia orange became naturalized and
all the trees you see are descendants from Mr. Judson's
baby. As everyone must know, the Washington Navel
orange is considered the best seedless fruit in all America.

The most picturesque of all Missions, if not the most
beautiful, is San Juan Capistrano, to which the swallows
return so faithfully and so punctiliously each year. Part of
it was destroyed in an earthquake in the early part of this
century, but the Church itself is still intact. There is, as
with other lovely California Missions, an atmosphere of
romance hovering over San Juan Capistrano. It is somewhat similar to that which is found at the old English and
French Abbeys. And many of the old Missions have the
same chequered history of those abroad. Like their ecclesiastic sisters, they were built in zeal and poverty. Then
came a rise to comparative affluence, ending in disintegration and abandonment. Happily some of those which fell
to ruin in California have been lovingly restored in the
manner of true piety.

The legend of the mythical Ramona touches here. Some
say that she was half-Irish and half-Indian, others that she
was pure Indian of the San Luis Rey tribe. Still others insist that she was the daughter of a Californian Mexican
named Gonzales. Indeed, the story of her life and her love
for her husband, Alessandro, is so human and takes on the
larger significance of a universality, that one sympathizes
with those who do not wish to believe that Ramona was

merely a fictive character out of the creative mind of Helen Hunt Jackson, the writer.

Her supposed places of residence are several. I have been shown her Adobe at Camulos (in Ventura County), and another at Gurjome (not far from San Juan Capistrano). After the publication of Mrs. Jackson's book a number of women impersonated her and she became what might be called the "Californian Anastasia." There are also various graves in Southern California where they tell you she was buried! Near Elsinore, named after that suspiciously modern Castle in Denmark which is said to contain the bones of Hamlet, there is enacted each year a Pageant of Ramona, telling the intriguing story of her life.

Critics of the book about her attacked it on the ground that the early Californian background which Mrs. Jackson used was quite unreal. I ask myself if perhaps I myself have used poetic licence in my descriptions of California's scenic beauty? Readers might well ask: does the State have any drawbacks? Yes it does. We have in some parts a nasty smog, sometimes called a high fog! There is a sudden change in temperature at eventide, a great differential between Noon and Night. During the dry season dust is prevalent in certain parts. Senior citizens may one day outnumber the Junior, and it has been called a place where old people go visit their parents! What's wrong with that?

You can put up with any demerits at such places as La Jolla (pronounced Hoya), an arm of land at sea a few miles from San Diego. It appeals to me as a small edition of Monte Carlo; there is the same lazy atmosphere, the same beckoning distances. There are, too, similar water grottoes, and for those who like caves there are intriguing examples on the beach—weirdly sculptured in disjointed vaultings by the soughing of the sea.

The Plymouth Rock of California is San Diego, also the Mother City of all Californian. The first white settlers landed here with Juan Cabrillo, as did Father Junipero Serra when he founded his first Mission where it still stands. It waits there for lovers of beauty, serenely watching the years pass as it witnesses many changes in its surrounding.

The *Frontera* of Mexico is so close that the feeling of being abroad is at its height. My advice is don't go there! The great sights of Mexico require a much longer trip into the interior. Towns such as Tiajuana are hardly more interesting than the Main Street section of Los Angeles!

My advice would be to go to Palm Springs, where trees whisper Arabia and flowers take on an uncanny beauty. Or to Indio to see the disciplined desert of date palms, whose sex life has been painstakingly described in book form. The Deglet Nur date was imported from Africa, and there is a suggestion of the Sahara as the white bells of the Yucca break the silence of the sands.

On any of the sagebrush territories you'll see small communities made up of people who have fallen victim of the desert's charms. They knew before they came that they would not discover gold, that it would offer little in food except what they brought with them. They have come here to find themselves, to conquer their own minds.

Or they just have something of the poet in them. The everchanging panorama of color in the Californian desert has been the theme for artists and poets since it was

discovered as a resort or retreat. None seems able to por-
tray the roseate hues of a desert sunrise or sunset. It is
well-nigh an impossible task ever to know the desert as a
piece of landscape. It is rather like understanding a
woman, the absolute knowing of whom seldom is. You
press hands, you touch lips—but you realize that a certain
gulf of loneliness circumscribes the soul from complete
knowledge. Yet the desert, like a woman, can reveal just
a little of her hidden soul to those who love her. The
colors are often of orgiastic sublimity.

My favorite desert is Death Valley, where the vegetation is of the classic type—thorny bushes, aloes, cactus
and mesquite, all useless to man, except for an occasional
yucca. It is the lowest part of the U.S.A. and from it you
can see Mount McKinley, the highest. Lizards, scorpions
and rattlesnakes, plus an occasional Coyote, were the
inheritors of this wilderness until man came and made it
habitable. It is now a State Park with an adequate number
of good hotels.

The macabre name was given it by some Forty-Niners
who were rescued from death when short-cutting through
the floor of the Valley to the Gold Fields, some of whom
lost their lives. Having crossed the Rocky Mountains in
carts drawn by cattle, all too frequently their only guide
was in the bleached bones of other men who had gone before and lost their way. First sight of it is like what one
imagines the surface of the Moon to be, so unbelievable
is it in appearance.

This extraordinary piece of natural phenomenon certainly has to be seen to be believed. It has been likened
to the Gobi Desert, and its temperature can be higher
than anywhere in Asia. In fact it has been in summer only

two degrees lower than that recorded anywhere else in the world—at Azizia in Libya. In winter the climate is ideal.

Like Los Angeles, Death Valley has yielded some fine fossils of the Oligocene and Miocene epochs and it is considered the greatest source of the Pleistocene (Ice) Age in the world. Only a few years ago the complete skeleton of a huge Rhinoceros was found in the red sand-stone cliffs, also several giant Mastadons.

In all the State Parks, and Death Valley is one of them, the Bear Flag is to be seen on the sign posts, and here is a story. It is said to have been designed by Lincoln Todd, a nephew of Abraham Lincoln, who is supposed to have cut it out of a red flannel petticoat of a Mexican lady who was handy when the emergency arose to create a flag. It has the image of a bear with a star in the upper left hand corner and Mr. Todd seems to have adapted it from the State flag of Texas.

In Astronomy the Bear is a symbol for a Constellation, implying an assembly. As you roam over the State, you become acquainted with the varying diversities of nationalities, such as Chinese, Japanese, Italian, Portuguese, Swiss, Hindus, Dutch, Korean, Slavs and Germans. In Fresno there is a large Armenian colony; and at Solvang (just over the mountains from Santa Barbara) the town is preponderantly Danish and is built in an architecture to suit them. Any representative convention of these men, who are mainly engaged in agriculture, would surely resemble a family reunion of the Tower of Babel!

You feel anything is possible for the future of California because, to paraphrase Shakespeare: Infinite variety cannot stale its custom. You see examples of villages that have grown into towns overnight, then into cities within a few years. You feel everywhere a sense of creative revolution in the State, compelling the world to a more natural outlook on life and its purposes. It could be that it will eventually generate the same spirit that made Italy and Spain nations of great artists and keen art lovers. It was in a similar climate, beside the waters of a sapphire sea—the same cloudless skies—that Spanish and Italian cities clustered, and their art was born.

An American Damascus   I. 3

FROM BENEATH A SPANISH HEAVEN YOU ARE only able to witness the past of two realms—the Moslem and the Christian; whereas at Santa Fé you have the quintessence of American History. You may read in scenes about you out there the periods of Spanish-Mexico, the Pagan, the Inquisition, and the final conquest by the United States. In fact, Santa Fé offers the gamut from the early Indian settlements through the Spanish and American military occupations up to the days of the Gold Rush and Buffalo Bill.

Here, indeed, is a setting as concentrated in history as Babylon or Damascus, with just as much an air of mystery one would sense at those historic places. And in this part of our Southwest it seems all the more vital under skies which might be likened to those of Andalusia. Immediately you arrive you feel that indefinable change—that fresh, wholesome snap that announces high altitudes.

The New Mexicans have a great sense of loyalty to their past and a proud feeling of inviolability of their soil. They have a reputation of being a little divorced from the realities of life, but they can be very practical when the need arises. They delight in sharing your joys, but they are ready to do this with your troubles, too. It is very easy to like them, also to quarrel with them—for they hold strong attitudes to religion and to politics. They are a curious cocktail of Mexican, Indian, and also just plain American, which somehow succeeds in making them hospitable and generous beyond the common.

If anyone wishes proof that Santa Fé is a God-fearing community, he need only reflect that there were eleven Churches in the territory before the *Mayflower* landed! San Miguel is believed to be the oldest in the United States. It was built in 1607, destroyed about seventy-five years later, and rebuilt in 1710. One of its bells, cast in Fourteenth Century Spain, is preserved within the Church, which stands in the heart of the city. The Cathedral of San Francisco dominates the town.

Paradoxically Santa Fé is the second youngest State Capital in the United States, but the oldest seat of government. The Governor's Palace has housed seventy-six Mexican and Spanish rulers, also nineteen American. Pedro de Perulta built his Capital here around 1606, calling it *La Villa Real de la Santa Fé de San Francisco de Assisi* (Royal City of the Holy Faith of Saint Francis of Assisi).

The Spanish invader built on the ruins of two Indian pueblos, when it was just known as the terminal of the

Old Transcontinental Trail—the most Northerly point to which the Spanish pressed in 1540. Thus the City has much ethnologic, historic, and prehistoric interest and was old before the Pilgrim Fathers fell on their knees (and then onto the aborigines!).

As a matter of fact, the Apache Indians conquered the Spanish in 1680 and occupied Santa Fé for twelve years. It has managed to keep remnants of the Indian, also signs of all the fluctuations necessary to change the atmosphere from a Spanish Province into its present Americanized status. In its gradual transition it has become just as individualistic as New Orleans.

What might be called *Renascence Adobe* architecture has been maintained. This is copied from the famous Governor's Palace, where General Lew Wallace wrote parts of *Ben Hur* during a tenure of office as Governor. Surrounded by the Ortiz, Sandia, and Sangre de Cristo Mountains, this gives a unique *cache*. Around the Plaza are good examples, such as the Art Museum. This fascinating building contains samples of six Spanish Missions now in ruins in the surrounding landscape. The lines of the Museum are gently flowing ones, none formally acute, which gives a pleasant sense of symmetry and a change of proportion at every aspect. Somehow, Adobe architecture fits better for a land where plains and mountains meet than any yet invented by modern man.

One of the strangest stories I have ever heard is told about the Chapel of Our Lady of Light at the Loretto Convent in Santa Fé. It concerns a gem-like mysterious-looking spiral staircase, such as one sees in Venetian Churches—and is therefore somewhat out of character with the Chapel, which was built in 1878. It takes the choristers to the Choir loft, and appeared—for one can hardly say it was constructed—quite some time after the building was completed.

The architect was also the builder, especially imported from Spain by the Bishop of Lamy. During the work the man lost his eyesight but nobly carried on, and it was not until he was on his way back to his country that the Nuns discovered to their dismay that he had neglected to install a staircase to the Choir loft. There was not enough money available to remedy this omission at once, so a ladder was substituted—which was hardly safe or satisfactory.

The good Nuns prayed to their Lady of Light for the necessary funds to come to them, but the religious community at that time was far from affluent, and there were many other pressing expenses. So when a very elderly bearded man appeared one day at the Convent gate and announced to the Mother Superior that he had come to build the forgotten staircase, everyone was in a state of anticipation. No one had ever seen the old man before and he was later described as looking like an Old Testament prophet, carrying an unattractive ragged bag of what was assumed to be carpentry tools—but no lumber. He refused to give his name except to say that he was *El Carpentero.*

All he asked was to be left alone in the Chapel, where he was for a period the Mother Superior stated could not have been longer than ten minutes. There was no sound of hammering or any noise at all; but when he emerged, he looked as if he had undergone great physical strain. With gracious old-world manners he beckoned the waiting

Nuns inside. One and all fell on their knees in prayers of gratitude for what met their eyes. Before their astonished gaze was the most beautiful circular staircase they had ever seen or imagined. In the words of one Nun, it was "a symbol of the ascent to Heaven."

The Mother Superior turned to thank the old carpenter, but he had disappeared as mysteriously as he had come. Investigation showed that the staircase was made of very highly polished wood not to be found anywhere in New Mexico and, moreover, put together without the use of nails or metal braces—seemingly woven in a way that nonplusses the observer.

Who could *El Carpentero* have been? Naturally enough the good Nuns of the Loretto Convent felt that their Patron Saint had sent the miraculous carpenter, St. Joseph. Who else would the Lady of Light use for such a holy mission but her own husband, the foster-father of Jesus Christ?

In addition to the religious climate of Santa Fé, you still find the self-sufficiency and independence of the early Amerind life untouched by the Nuclear or Machine Age, disproving what historians like Toynbee have tried to establish—that civilizations do not get a second chance! The plateau scenery of New Mexico is not a little Biblical and has been likened to the Holy Land. The motorist may see moving pictures of peaceful pastoral scenes as he glides along, enhanced by the spectacular grandeur of erosion formations.

Above all he will see sunsets beyond compare. These are subject to certain electrifying phenomena which give off a strangely beautiful coloring. The dying rays of the

sun seemingly fall aslant so that the horizon blazes with
numerous tints of purple and violet. This mirage effect
brings to mind the Keatsian lines that it

> Oft-times hath
> Charmed magic casements opening on the foam
> Of perilous seas, in faery lands forlorn.

The Lost Grave of Columbus   I. 4

As a GRATEFUL AMERICAN CITIZEN, I WAS
thinking lately that I would like to make a pilgrimage to
the grave of Christopher Columbus. One pertinent book
of reference told me that his remains lie in the Havana
Cathedral, another that his last resting place is to be found
in the Cathedral of Santo Domingo.

One would have thought that there would be no doubt
about the shrine of the most famous man in the world,
whose voyage of discovery in those tiny ships and their
long struggle of buffeting Atlantic waves, makes one of
the great stories in all literature. Some parts are sad, others
very amusing—how he became stuck in the seaweed of
the Sargasso Sea for two weeks; or when he duped the
natives of Jamaica into giving him supplies by threatening
them that the Moon would lose its light, knowing that an
eclipse was due; or the time when his sailors choked on
those cheroots they gave them; and those footprints of the

alligator which they mistook for a dog who might be guarding hidden gold! All these made up a medley of farces and ironies—until the Great Discoverer was led through the streets of Madrid in chains.

Like the muddle over his remains, there is no exact record of his death. This is supposed to have occurred on May 20, 1506, at Valladolid, where he had gone to plead for the restoration of his confiscated property. We know that he made this last voyage sometime in 1504, but by the time he arrived at Valladolid his friend, Queen Isabella, on whom he relied for mediation, had died. Apparently he lingered there for about eighteen months, more and more discouraged by the way the Court officials fobbed him off.

It seems inconceivable that this great genius of a navigator, who had shown such faith and perseverance for Spain, would have to die disabused and alone. But his voyages had been projected as a gamble in which he was thought to have failed. They were assessed without anticipation of the colonization which followed his daring.

It was not until twenty-eight days after his death that a brief bulletin was issued by Royal Order stating "Admiral Christopher Columbus is dead." His son, Diego, came three years later and supervised the removal of his father's body to the Carthusian Vaults in Seville Cathedral, where the impoverished Admiral wished to be laid.

When Ferdinand, his last surviving son, died quite some time later, he asked that his body and that of his father and brother be transported and laid within the Cathedral of Isabel la Nueva in Santo Domingo, the island which first established the existence of a Western Hemisphere— proof of his father's geographical opinions.

Sometime before 1549 this was accomplished, but without any record. Writing in that year, the Archbishop of the newly completed and consecrated Cathedral in Santa Domingo, one Alonso de Fuenmayor, noted that the tomb of the great Admiral Columbus was in his care and that the "case in which his bones lie is greatly venerated and respected."

There they remained intact until the year 1795 when Santo Domingo became a Republic and the Spanish Government ordered them to be taken and placed in Havana Cathedral for safer keeping. Removal was probably in secret because of the revolutionary times, and there was considerable schism between Church and the new State. A marble slab was erected in the Cuban Cathedral noting the bones of Christopher Columbus had been reinterred, and that was that. Thousands of tourists of the island have been shown the shrine of the Great Discoverer.

However, in September 1877 an event occurred that proved that the Spanish Government had unwittingly perpetrated one of the greatest funereal blunders in History. The Rector of Santo Domingo Cathedral was supervising some alteration operations near the Sacristy for the opening of a door which had been walled up a long time before. In removing some stones a niche was discovered containing two leaden cases and an empty space where one had been removed. Both were engraved with corroded lettering, but with careful cleaning this was deciphered. Thrilled almost to the point of tears, the Rector read: "El Almirante, Don Luis Colon." There was other lettering which was illegible.

Realizing that the discovery would lead to a serious controversy, the Rector awaited the return of the Archbishop, who was absent at that time. Later, at a formal gathering presided over by the President of the Dominican Republic and attended by his Cabinet and all foreign diplomats, the leaden case was opened. It contained a human skeleton in jumbled bones, and inside the lid of the case they read:

ILLtre y ESdo VARON dn CRISTOVAL COLON
(Illustrious and renowned man Christopher Columbus)

Spellbound, this group of distinguished men stood there silent. It was the Spanish Ambassador who broke it, claiming the case and contents in the name of Spain. He insisted that they be sent immediately to Havana, at that time still a Royal possession. The President's answer was a firm and laconic NO.

In retaliation the King of Spain sent an investigator, a renowned archaeologist, who declared the discovery a forgery. The Spanish Ambassador accused the Archbishop of trying to make an American Mecca in the Dominican Republic.

The matter reached the proportions of an International incident. Finally it was conceded by unbiased judges that the Spanish mission, that had been entrusted to reinter the bones of Columbus in Havana, had taken the wrong remains, those of his son, Diego Columbus.

In a larger sense the mistake was symbolic of the error Columbus had himself made, thinking that his discovery of Santo Domingo was that of the Indies. Who could have foreseen that this alone would ultimately lead others into those regions he was convinced existed? America is the real monument to him whether his bones lie in Santo

Domingo Cathedral or somewhere else. It is in America
that his memory will live forever, as fadeless and immortal.

Columbus discovered Puerto Rico as well as the Virgin
Islands, and it seems proper that these islands are now
owned by the United States. Puerto Rico was awarded to
us in 1898 at the Treaty of Paris, after the Spanish-Ameri-
can War. The adjoining Virgin Islands were purchased by
us for twenty-five million dollars from the Government
of Denmark in 1916.

Their name must have piqued curiosity for many years,
also must have been the subject for numerous jokes. The
only one I can think of was that witticism attributed to
Disraeli. Asked in Parliament to say where they were on
the map, he replied: "I cannot say exactly, but I'm sure
they are nowhere near the Isle of Man!"

It is possible that the Virgin Islands were named by
Columbus himself, for he named a number of other Carib-
bean islands, always mindful of religious significance. It is
said they were christened in memory of Ursala, an early
Christian martyress who was murdered with several hundred other virgins by the Huns. Paradoxically, one has
been rechristened *Dead Man's Chest* because it looks like
a coffin seen at a distance. This particular islet suggested
to Robert Louis Stevenson the first line of his famous poem
"Fifteen men on a deadman's chest."

Not many people know that the term "Black Irish" origi-
nated in these islands. Oliver Cromwell sent many an
Irishman into life-long exile here. They were allowed to
bring no women and so they propagated with the natives.
Their descendants have Irish names and speak with strong
Irish brogues. This once so baffled a visitor from Dublin

who felt sure they must have been born there. Tactfully, he asked a native how long he had been on the particular island. Actually the man had come from a neighboring one, and so he replied, "About three years, Sir."

The Irishman was flabbergasted. "And does it take so short a time for the sun to turn you black?" he queried.

Christopher Columbus certainly named Montserrat, which lies lower down on the Archipelago. He called it after the Monastery of that name in the Black Virgin district of Catalania, where St. Ignatius of Loyola once resided.

As a final link with the mainland of America, Alexander Hamilton was born at Nevis, another of the islands in the group called the Leewards. And appropriately enough it was a violent storm that made possible his emigration to the United States and his subsequent participation in the stormy furies of the American Revolution. Not generally known is the fact that he wrote a vivid description of a West Indian hurricane for the local paper. This piece attracted such notice by people who were quick to recognize good writing that they made plans for sending him to the mainland for further education.

To return to the grave of Columbus, his bones are now suspended in an elaborate marble memorial at Santo Domingo in what is now called the Columbus Cathedral, the cornerstone of which was laid by his son, Diego, in 1514. No words are needed to tell visitors that the whole outward and onward movement of the Great Exploring Age was set in motion by him. To those who may add that it would have happened later on without him, one can only insist that through him it resulted.

Facaetiae Americana   I. 5

AMERICA'S FIRST COMIC PAPER WAS NOT PUB-
lished until 1876. Serious papers had, of course, published
jokes much earlier. A quick look at some of these proves
that the humor of the times was blithe and generous—
often arising from the stupidity of man. Its philosophy
stressed that a world without a little stupidity would be
a sorry one indeed. Gradually, however, American humor
shaped itself to a type all its own, as a subtle touchstone
of the mind thrown out to test one's mood. Contrasted
with that of England, which aims at being an affair of the
head, American humor was and still is an affair of the
heart. What is the wisecrack but a spiritual release from
the depths of the subconscious? It is a smiling away of
troubles.

Kidding is an American speciality and is considered an
indication of friendship, much misunderstood by foreigners. When Oscar Wilde came to this country in 1882 he
was at his wildest, firing witticisms broadside. He cut
a very flamboyant figure, with his long, wavy hair, and
dressed nattily in black suiting with a multi-colored waist-
coat and shirt festooned with diamonds. No one knew
better how to use his eccentricities effectively for publicity purposes, and all went well with his lecture tour
until he reached Denver.

There he was victimized by some real kidding from Eugene Field, the American poet, also a gifted farceur and the owner of a very waggish sense of humor. He decided to take Oscar down a peg or two, and he hit on a most jocular plan. Announcing to the press that Oscar would arrive a day earlier, Field feigned the arrival of the great Oscar Wilde, driving from the railway station in an open four-in-hand, complete with flaxen wig, sporting a sunflower—sneering arrogantly in the Wilde manner, to the plaudits of the waiting crowds.

Later, when Wilde did arrive he was treated as an impostor. Utterly failing to see the funny side, he was furious that his thunder had been stolen. Years later, when Field went to London, he took his revenge and tried to ruin the American's reputation as a poet.

Most people remember General Douglas MacArthur's triumphant return to America in 1953, after ten years of duty in the Orient. These were without any break in his absence from U.S.A. due to his onerous duties, and he felt keenly a nostalgia for his country.

During his service as Supreme Commander of the Allies, he passed five years in Tokyo. To relax he would sometimes take his wife to some of the surrounding landmarks, and among these he became especially fascinated by the volcano called *Bandai-san*, which stands about one hundred and twenty-five miles north of the city.

The General was most interested in the coned peak, collecting all the startling facts about it. He would tell friends, whom he took there, how it had erupted ferociously in 1888 and had blown off the side of the nearby peak named *Kohandi*, removing, as it did so, one hundred million tons of earth. He also stressed the fact that *Bandai-san* was seventy thousand and five years old.

Just before he was recalled to America, he took a party of visiting friends to see the smoldering volcano he knew so well. As the party gazed from the top into the mysteries of the crater, MacArthur began his usual spiel, ending as usual with the age of it.

"How can you be so accurate, General?" asked one of his friends.

"Because," he replied incisively, "they told me five years ago that *Bandai-san* is seventy thousand years old—and I've been here that number of years myself!"

John Hanson:
First President of U.S.A.?

CURIOUS COINCIDENCES EXIST IN AMERICAN
History. There were two prominent Benedict Arnolds.
One was the infamous traitor. The other, his great-grand-
father (1615-1678), three times Governor of Rhode Island
—a kindly and beloved man, who was a master of all the
Indian dialects in his demesne. Then, there are the strange
death-patterns of John Adams, the second President, and
Thomas Jefferson, the third. Both men died on the same
day, July 4, 1826—exactly fifty years after the great document they shared in creating was ratified in the Continental Congress.

More than coincidence, I feel, is the historical amnesia
suffered by President John Hanson of that Congress. He
was the first to give the Presidential service after it was
federalized in 1781, which year he was elected. Any student of American History knows that there were two other
Presidents of the Continental Congress before him and
that none possessed executive powers. But the year Hanson served, it had begun representation for all the States,
and the word *United* was added. He became known as
the President of the United States, and it is a matter of
record that General Washington addressed him as "Mr.

President." He spoke to him thus when he reported on the Victory of Yorktown to the Congress.

This interesting American leader has, I believe, been made the subject of a conspiracy to forget him in order to consolidate the idolization of one man as first President. But his death in history is unfinished while there is someone to remember him. I include this piece well aware that controversy has raged from time to time among scholars as to whether he had a claim to be called first President or an historical mountebank.

Unfortunately Washington's diary for 1781 mysteriously disappeared after being loaned to his first biographer. This might have revealed a rapport between the two men. Let his record speak for itself: During President Hanson's busy year in office, he started what became the Federal Reserve Banking System, ushered in diplomatic relationships with Sweden and Holland, and—perhaps most important of all—established a Post Office Department for the United States.

John Hanson passed an Act establishing a line of express posts between New Hampshire and Georgia, which were gradually extended elsewhere. This linked the United States for many years, but mails moved very slowly. It was not until 1858, however, that the Pony Express was founded, as a private company. These riders galloped in relays and fought Indians out West, often making three hundred miles a day—for which they got paid at the rate of $5.00 per ounce! (The Pony Express was never part of the Post Office Department of the United States—mistakenly believed by many Hollywood script writers.)

Rightly or wrongly, I hope that this forgotten American leader is worth a few minutes of our time. He was born

in 1715 in Prince George's County, Maryland, in which
State his name is written large on every page of its history,
before his rise to fame as America's first President. He
was always a modest man, whose modesty was surely only
equalled by his love for his country. During the struggle
for liberty, he was the leader in every important movement made in his own State—movements which helped
to lay the foundations of American freedom.

The claim of John Hanson as first President has been
dismissed by contemporary historians because they insist
George Washington was the first under the new order of
the Federal Constitution of 1787. But is this correct?
Abraham Lincoln said in a speech on May 4th, 1861:
"The Union is much older than the Constitution. This
was formed in 1774, matured and continued in the Declaration of Independence; then further matured and continued in the faith of all the thirteen States, expressly
plighted in 1781."

He was, of course, referring to the life of the body
called the Continental Congress known as "The United
States in Congress Assembled," which had its headquarters in Philadelphia. (The meaning of the word Continental was the popular term for the Colonies as a unit.)
And John Hanson was elected President of that body in
1781, the year the Articles of Confederation were signed
—giving each State equal representation. Surely this is
the year when the United States attained its majority as
a nation and marked the great turning point in history.
The Articles of the new Federalized Congress influenced
the basic laws of the United States.

For John Hanson the equality of man was no mere
political dogma but a practical code which governed him

in all his relations of life. In 1775 he had been the prime mover in the Continental Congress to make one of its first pieces of legislature a Department of Indian Affairs. This set up three departments designated northern, middle, and southern, with a commissioner for each. The first commissioners were Patrick Henry and Benjamin Franklin.

Disputants to the claim for him to be considered first President further say that he was not elected by a democratic system. Neither was George Washington! Both men were elected by Congress, and in all the records of the federalized Continental Congress Hanson is referred to as the President of the United States of America.

In his year of office he selected the design of the United States Seal, still in use—an eagle holding an olive branch in its beak. He also signed the edict making the federal Thanksgiving Day the last Thursday of November and he was in office when the first Fourth of July was observed as a federal holiday.

Relations with George Washington appear to have been cordial. Hanson's son was assistant private secretary to him during several military campaigns. But the record revealing the association of the two men is missing in the lost diary. Washington kept his diary carefully and said frankly what he felt about his associates. It is odd that the biographer, probably the idolizing Parson Weems, returned those for the other years. Even more strange is the fact that no biographer afterwards ever mentioned the name of John Hanson.

Could it be that the feeling was that deification could be better achieved for the Father of His Country by no competition from the man who was technically an earlier first President? Was there not even a time when this deification became so pressing that George Washington scornfully refused an offer to make him King of America?

President Hanson died in 1783 and lies buried next to his wife in Oxon Hill Cemetery, Maryland. Though forgotten and ignored, he is "an inseparable part of the inseparable union of inseparable States."

Olde Virginea   II. 2

BEFORE I CAME TO AMERICA, MY FIRST INTERest was stimulated by reading Thackeray's famous book *The Virginians*. I pictured the State in my young mind as a country of gentle undulations, where rivers flow quietly in winding curves—a land well-timbered by restful trees. I saw it with a landscape of pervading harmony made up of fields decorated by grazing cattle, under a softly clouded sky.

Thirty years later I made my first trip there and noted how well I had sensed Virginia's Arcadian charm. I was, however, surprised to find it not to be a land of eternal summer, for from the perspective of England the product of tobacco suggested to me a tropical climate. It came as a surprise that its unchanging agriculture is responsive to the rounds of the seasons.

I'm sure that every new visitor revels in Virginia's old world charm. The stories of the early pioneers contain the ingredients of true romance, if only for the great courage of the men and women who filled the stage. Some of the forests that preside darkly in the distances rival in magnificence and age such covers as Sherwood Forest, and would make an even safer hiding place for Robin Hood and company.

The towns and countryside exhale the charm of North Wales. Commenting on this to an old gaffer I met in Fredericksburg as I revelled there for the first time, his answer fell like stones: "You see," he explained, as if Virginia's charm could be brought down to a common denominator, "the North never left us enough money for vulgarity!"

This mental civil war goes on, and it is really manifesting the special pride in being Southern. Can one blame Virginians for being proud of such an enviable heritage of history and beauty? The South is an atmosphere and you feel it keenly immediately you enter Dixie. You come to places like Fredericksburg with a sense of pilgrimage, to visit its battle-fields and shrines. It was named after the son of George the Second, a Prince of Wales. Incorporated in 1727, after being founded a few years earlier by a Leaseland Grant, there still exists a sentimental link with England.

The surrounding countryside is so composed and dreamlike that it is hard to realize so many parts of it once were scenes of frightful human slaughter in the worst Civil War the world has ever known. Whatever the issue, you know from hearing of the carnage that the price was one we cannot afford to pay again—even if it did give America an opportunity to test her faith and explore her soul.

Being between the Confederate and Federal Capitals,

it is easy to see why Fredericksburg was put into the fiercest fighting. Happily these once-bloodstained fields of Chancellorsville and Spotsylvania are as pleasantly peaceful today as are those of Leipzig and Waterloo—with the scars of war obliterated by the same placid agriculture.

All unhappy memories are far outweighed all over the State by the sight of lovely colonial mansions which dot the landscape. Many of these stately homes take rank with some of the great ones of England and France. At Fredericksburg, for instance, the "Big House" is the former home of Colonel and Mrs. Fielding Lewis, where George Washington passed some of his happiest hours with his favorite sister, Mrs. Lewis. *Kenmore* divines his presence for you in a rather special informal way. Here you see him life-size; whereas at other shrines he is too immense. There is an intimacy at *Kenmore* which makes you feel mind-to-mind with the Great Man, as you picture him romping with the children of the house. It was here that he passed several Christmases.

Now a museum, of which the townspeople are the pious wardens, *Kenmore* was saved from a sentence of demolition forty years ago when two patriotic Virginia ladies— Mrs. H. H. Smith and her mother Mrs. V. K. Fleming— miraculously raised the necessary funds in short order for its continued existence as a shrine.

The Masonic Cemetery of Fredericksburg contains one of the strangest American graves I have ever come across in U.S.A. You read on an imposing headstone that it was erected to the memory of Lewis Littlepage (1762-1802), an American soldier-adventurer. He served as a high-ranking officer in the Army of Russia's Catherine the Great. Later he was in the employ of King Stanislas of Poland, who raised him to the rank of Chamberlain. He returned from Europe to Fredericksburg in his fortieth year to die, and gossip of a peculiar kind is still heard about him locally, implying that he rivalled Casanova in his amatory adventuring with at least one ruling European Queen.

Just a short piece away from this tranquillizing spot is the James Monroe Law Office, containing the same furniture used by President Monroe when he was incumbent at the White House—including the desk on which he signed the famous doctrine which bears his name. Close by is the Rising Sun Tavern, once a rialto for celebrated men and the setting where Jefferson and his committee drafted his bill of religious freedom. Mercer's Apothecary, a shrine to a hero and close friend of Washington, should be seen, too.

In Virginia it is borne in upon one that three of the greatest documents of American heritage were produced by her sons. It is the universality of mind that these men exhaled, the audacity of their political imagination, that claims them for the world at large. There was the little-known *Declaration of Rights* issued by Edmund Pendleton in 1776; the *Bill of Rights* drafted by George Mason and now part of the Constitution itself—and lastly the *Declaration* formulated largely by Thomas Jefferson.

What a role the banks of the softly-flowing Rappahannock River has played in both Revolutionary and Civil Wars, also in many a skirmish with the Indians—as told by Captain John Smith. It is truly a piece of liquid history.

Indeed, in the State of Virginia you may, if you wish, go further back than civilized history. Not far from Fredericksburg, below Richmond, there are two ancient homes which crossed the Atlantic brick-by-brick. Now known as *Virginia House,* the *Priory of the Holy Sepulcher* was originally built by the first Earl of Warwick in 1125 A.D. This lovely ecclesiastic building was converted by Thomas Hawkins in 1565, who lived in it at Warwick. It was occupied by other families throughout several hundred years until, in 1925, it was purchased from the housewrecker and shipped to a Virginian.

In its native prime many notable personalities greeted the halls and on one occasion Queen Elizabeth the First held Court there. As proof of this, her Coat of Arms is carved on a stone in the front hall. The stately old home blends into the local scene as if it had been planted there. Its twin, *Agecroft Hall,* was brought piecemeal the same year from Lancashire in England. It was built originally in pre-Elizabethan times for a family named Langley in the quaint timber-and-plaster style with leaded casements. The garden is said to be a simulacrum of that seen at Hampton Court Palace near London.

Interesting homes abound in Virginia. There is the *Nelson House* at Yorktown; *Stratford* in Westmoreland County (the home of the Robert E. Lee family); *Gunston Hall,* where George Mason once lived; and *Westover* on the James River, homestead of the Byrds—and crowning them all is *Monticello,* high on its windswept hill-top, preserved just as Jefferson left it the day he died there.

The State Capital of Richmond has suggestions of ancient Greece, with its Capitol building fashioned after the *Maison Carré,* one of the finest Grecian temples in perfect preservation in Nîmes, Southern France. The Colonial style house has borrowed, too, from the Greek, with windows balanced by other windows of same shape and size. This *motif* blends gracefully into Richmond's hilly nature.

Old Broad Street, in Richmond, brims with history. Here is the Church where Patrick Henry worshipped with his family in Pew Number 72; and it was here that he delivered his speech about liberty and death. He later became the first Governor of Virginia, reelected in 1784.

No lover of American History should miss the experience of re-creating the past at Williamsburg, so named after William the Third. Eighty of the original buildings still stand from the hundreds that were needed to be demolished and restored in 1927. The Virginia Assembly still meets one session a year in the Old Capital Building from where the Declaration of Independence was first proclaimed.

Of all attractions to Virginia, I have been most fascinated by the Natural Bridge, bought by Thomas Jefferson for twenty shillings in 1774. A solid mass of limestone without a break and carved by Nature out of a bed which once covered the whole region, this colossal phenomenon looks like some huge prehistoric castle. It is perfectly placed at the extremity of a deep chasm through which Cedar Creek gently flows. Even today one cannot improve upon the description Henry Clay gave of the Bridge; "A gigantic crossing not made with hands, that spans a river, carries a highway, and makes two mountains one."

Boston: The Future of the Past   II. 3

A NEW GUIDE BOOK TO THE "ATHENS OF America" informs us that the old tradition of the city has died to a large extent. Instead of being populated, as of old, by superior people derived from old world stock— people who had at least one *Mayflower* ancestor—things have changed. "Recent statistics prove," continues this informant, "that Boston is now one third foreign born and therefore three quarters un-English by descent. The City today is mainly run by a predominantly Irish population . . ."

After such an unkindly innuendo, dare I say that I have always regarded Boston as a suburb of Connemara? I also realize that my race cannot be all things to all men, and I am reminded of when Eamon de Valera was speaking in Boston in 1919, fund-raising for the Irish Fight for Freedom.

Among several he touched upon, his main theme was on how Ireland could be made a self-governing country. "What we want is an Irish Republic," he cried.

"Oh, no we don't," shouted back a Boston diehard. "We've got one here already!"

With a certain amount of justice, no other city in the world is more conscious of its rarefied origin. It is the past to which Boston essentially belongs, and no flood of foreign immigration is likely to obliterate it. Its memories, like its street names, are of England old and New. To wander about Boston offers something like what one imagines England of the Eighteenth Century was like. You need not travel far into the Blue Hills to survey a scene which the Pilgrim Fathers would have recognized.

Any Frenchman or Englishman can come to Boston to revel in this old world charm, can feel a familiar environment. Like so many provincial towns in England and France, the streets twist and wind. An Englishman might liken Beacon Street, bordering on the Common, to the lazy part of Piccadilly fronting Green Park in London. And Boston Common might suggest Hyde Park to him, the same natural beauty only time can confer—the same broad spaces, the shades of old trees overlooking ponds of water.

For three hundred and fifty years the Common has been the rialto for Bostonians, and it is hallowed by History. Here the tragedies and comedies of an eventful period were enacted. Malefactors were hanged, witches burned. There gallants walked with their dames, observed disdainfully by Puritans.

Somehow Boston resembles an elderly lady who has outlived her contemporaries. You can picture her turning over a handful of dusty relics and old photographs, a widow who has inherited the business acumen of her deceased successful husband. If only she can continue letting things develop by themselves, allow that *laisser-faire* to function (as the French do) in order to preserve that air she has created of old-fashioned festivity.

In Boston there are yet places where you may wander and find that unique, precious beauty born of accident and surprise. There are still streets that are more than just a thoroughfare. You never know in these just what may confront you if you turn a corner, nor what century you may be thrust into. Here is an old farmhouse type of house that might have been built by the first settlers; over there several Eighteenth Century red brick homes. You feel that wonderful diversity springing from natural transition.

Many modern houses have not been compelled to follow a hard, immovable line. Some are covered with Virginia creeper, adding a charm to the most commonplace. In Boston it is borne in upon one that city architecture is the most English in America. It ought surely to be a matter of congratulation on the stroke of luck that saved it from the influence of Jacobean and Tudor patterns, which would never fit in. Fortunately, the *Mayflower* sailed from England after this ugly period came to a close, and instead you find houses influenced by the art of Wren and Inigo Jones, but with no absurd mimicry, no prejudiced obedience to their ideas. It is a style which is sufficiently original to be considered American, but it leaves one with the feeling the builders wanted just enough of English style to keep the memory here.

Harvard Medical School is a fine building modelled on Classic Greek. Mrs. Eddy's Mother Church is in Italian Renascence. Inevitably one visits the homes of Emerson and Thoreau, both of which reflect the background for these great writers excellently. All of us have a way of fixing in our mind's eye an abiding place for famous writers, and I find I have always seen these poets here —with a glimpse of Thoreau at Walden as a brief exception.

The lover of the past can come to Boston and let his imagination revel in the lovely old buildings. It is the

loving respect shown by Americans to their historical
buildings which impresses every European visitor. The
Old South Meeting House is given a warm-hearted venera-
tion. Not an episode of the City's history is unconnected
with it. It is the psychological center of the City, no
matter how much it becomes enmeshed in progress. It
stands on the site of John Winthrop's garden and is rich
in the memory of Increase and Cotton Mather. Within its
walls Benjamin Franklin was christened, the famous Boston Tea Party planned. From here those "Mohawks" made
their way to the Harbor to see how tea mixed with salt
water, although the actual spot today has been reclaimed
and is now dry land.

Faneuil Hall (named after a Huguenot merchant who
gave it to the City in 1742) might be a Town Hall in any
English city borough. It is essentially English inside and
out. It is a fitting symbol of a city that continues to blend
commerce and enterprise with the worship of tradition.
It is truly part of America's past—or is it the future?

Some Experimental Utopias   II. 4

IF EQUALITY OF RELIGION IS ONE OF AMERICA'S
achievements, much credit for it must be given to the non-
existence of an Established Church—so common to European countries. One feels in America the sentiment that

religion was made for man, not man for religion, and perhaps that is why a church embraces social amenities that are unknown elsewhere. Is there any other country where the Church forms an outer circle which is not at all "churchy"? Visitors are amazed when they find that churches in America promote social enjoyments, such as plays and musicals, and even Halloween parties. Some of them rejoice that Religion is throwing aside some of its impedimenta and is gradually abandoning uncompromising dogmas and hidebound attitudes.

We are perhaps reaching the more intelligent approach —that Religion should be concerned more with conduct here and now, rather than with the Future State, which will take care of itself if conduct is right. In this we are merely following the stricture of the Saint nicknamed the *Little Flower,* who felt it best to spend her Heaven doing good on earth.

The Religion of the Future will surely start in America and will accordingly correspond with the moral and material needs of a changing world. Let us hope it will soon be born. Meanwhile, the romantic stories of those many nineteenth century religious groups who came to the United States to found their own utopias make fascinating reading, if only because they have been forgotten. These people came in search of unobstructed skies, where they would be let alone with their ideals and be allowed to live apart. They learned that no man can be an island.

All the same, the story of these noble experiments, with all their deep and absorbing struggle, is part of the American Story. Their inspirations were communitarian, organized according to Acts 2:32-37, 45-46—which propounds the basis for owning things in common. Theirs was a revolt of the soul, similar to that which brought the Founding Fathers much earlier.

One of the most interesting of these sects was called the Separatists of Zoar, Ohio, originally formed by Jacob Boehm (1575-1624) whose writings were the basis for the philosophy of the group. In Germany they made themselves unpopular with the *status quo* religious leaders because they refused to comply with the rituals of Baptism or Confirmation. The members also refused to take part in military activity and, in fact, refused to acknowledge any government superior to their own.

The last leader of the Separatists was Jacob Bimeler, who was a homeopathic doctor, as well as being a physician of the soul. He was an angry disputant of society, a Utopian visionary. In his boyhood he had read the story of Robinson Crusoe, also the adventures of the Jesuit missionaries who crossed the sea. Through these his fancy caught fire and he wished to find some sequestered place in the New World, some colony where his followers could get away from a corrupt civilization—somewhere peaceable, and free.

Jacob Bimeler was a man of astute business acumen and he was clever in urging his ideas on people of influence. Aided by the Society of Friends, he and his disciples took ship for America, arriving in Philadelphia in August, 1817. Their ship proved to be most unseaworthy and gave them all a harrowing voyage. Bimeler needed all the spiritual powers he could muster to keep up the lagging spirits of his flock, and to his credit, he won an exalted position in their hearts for the way he bolstered them.

They settled temporarily in Philadelphia while seeking

permanent headquarters. After diligent searching, he found them the ideal spot to begin building their dream-colony—six thousand acres in the wilderness of Ohio which he bought very cheaply with money loaned without interest by the Quakers.

Rather similar to the lovely Black Forest near Württemberg, from where they had come, the land was covered with primeval forests. Thick snow covered the ground when the first settlers arrived there in March, 1818. Floods engulfed their first efforts at building and spring came late that year with a chill in the air. Bimeler was a born leader, however, and therefore the most impersonal of thinkers. If he was an idealist whose dreams and visions were inspired by the intellect, he also had that rare gift of imparting affection and at the same time rendering his people slaves to his will. In an amazingly short time the Separatists had built the town they named Zoar, in honor of Lot who fled to the city of that name in the Biblical story.

According to Bimeler, the germs of new spiritual growths were in the soil and all of them prayed that Zoar would be a refuge from the evils they had left behind in Europe. Besides ordinary agrarian pursuits they began raising flax for such industries as linen and matting. Bimeler occupied what was called the King's Palace, which may be seen at Zoar to this day and now contains examples of their pottery, furniture and musical instruments, which they were later to manufacture.

Zoarite products became known and the colony prospered, selling their wares far and wide. When the railway came and their market was invaded by larger producers, the manufacture of furniture was commenced as well as pottery out of the local mud, which proved excellent for this new industry. The furniture was of a specialized kind, such as no other manufacturer of the times was turning out. Some of these pieces are collector's items today.

Under Bimeler's Charter of 1819 the Separatists agreed to "unite themselves in the Apostolic sense, through the communion of property . . ." They promised faithful obedience, agreeing to settle any differences by arbitration. They further promised not to make any claim against the Colony if they ever decided to leave it. And in eighty years of its life there were very few desertions—but also hardly any converts.

No plans appear to have been made for Bimeler's successor. Even so, he always taught that life without death would be a drama without conclusion. Man's destiny, he argued, rested on four great realities: Life, Death, Joy, and Pain, and it is impossible to isolate one from the other and avoid a conflict—which is, he insisted, the essence of human existence.

He continued to administer the Colony for exactly thirty-five years after he and his followers had arrived at Philadelphia. He was their medical doctor, governor and business executive. So when he died on August 10, 1853 it is not surprising that there was no one to take his place. By 1898 the Separatist Society had become so separated that the population declined to the point it had to be dissolved. The assets were divided equally by those who had been loyal, sharing in a sum over one million dollars.

If you go to Zoar today, you may see the garden Bimeler designed, in the center of the existing village. It is a miniature replica of the New Jerusalem described in Revelations (21-22). Radiating from the Tree of Life, in geometric pattern there are twelve shrubs (the Apostles) which define twelve paths (the Tribes of Israel). It is said that some of Zoar's present citizens still live comfortably on the funds inherited from their forebears, and Bimeler's business shrewdness.

The Harmonists of Economy, Pennsylvania, are sometimes called the Rappites because their story really propels around their leader, George Rapp, a very considerable leader, too. He was the son of poor farming folks in Southern Germany. As a young man he evidenced a grave and dreamy personality and became dissatisfied with the Lutherian doctrines of his own religion. He was at heart a sociologist and found himself unable to reconcile his own way of life with the sociology of the New Testament.

He believed in a spiritual power of his own concept, linking it with the common will. He believed this empiric force directed humanity just as the will directs the body —and this cosmos was, like the soul, invisible. Modern life had dehumanized man and he felt the task before him was to rehumanize mankind.

George Rapp married a farmer's daughter and at first they lived contented in an unchanging agriculture, realizing that the things of the soil are forever. He distinguished himself in the district as a lay preacher, driving in the message of the soil with an eloquence that held his audience rapt. As he was not ordained, the meetings were held in his own home; later he hired a hall and came to the attention of the Bishopric. A mild persecution followed.

Truth was the demand and the necessity of his mind. New religious theories came to him and seemingly claimed George Rapp for their interpreter. One day he was visited

upon by a portent which informed him that Christ would
make a reappearance in the United States, and that he
had been chosen to make preparations to receive Him.
The portent also stated that the United States was the
only country exempt from the dismal prophesies of the
Bible.

Rapp's belief that America was the land where the Religion of the Future would be born became an obsession.
He fired enough enthusiasm into a sufficient number of
followers to make plans to go there. Funds were raised for
him and his wife (plus an assistant) to sail for America
to explore for a suitable location to found a colony for the
Harmonists, as they were now called.

They arrived safely and without incident in the summer
of 1803 at the Port of Baltimore. After much exploration
for a site, they settled on five thousand odd acres of un-
improved land in the Valley of the Connoquenessing.
Rapp returned to Europe in order to organize things to
bring back the rest of his group. His assistant was left in
charge of his wife and young son. This young man turned
out to have remarkable qualities which led Rapp to adopt
him and he later became known as Frederick Rapp.

In due course, Rapp returned with three hundred Harmonists, arriving auspiciously enough on July 4th, 1804
on a worthy bark named the *Aurora*. Many were skilled
in certain trades and all brought with them their life
savings, which were pooled in a common fund. Fired by
Rapp's fine enthusiasm, they all got to work.

To understand the inspiration with which these people
accomplished so much, it is necessary to know something
of Rapp's spell-binding power. He always spoke with eyes

heavenward and with a melodious voice—as a soul to souls. His words were always grave and plain, pressed home with the force of their reality. He aimed never to display, always to convince. He marshalled his arguments with the skill of a tactician. And he managed to reach the heart by a wise knowledge of its processes.

It is not surprising, therefore, that we find built in the first year fifty log cabins, a church, a schoolhouse, a grist-mill, a saw-mill, a tannery, and a huge storehouse for grain. Among the crops harvested were rye, hemp, corn, flax, and wheat. Not just a few fields, but many.

Everything was going so well when Rapp's strange religious beliefs came to the fore. He now declared that Adam was a dual being, who was created with both sexual elements. Because of this, he insisted, Adam could have increased his species without the aid of woman if he had been content with this state—and the Fall of Man could thus have been avoided! So Rapp issued a new Commandment for his people: "Thou shalt not covet thy neighbor's wife nor thy own." In short, he imposed immediate celibacy on every Harmonist, including himself. News of this reached England where Lord Byron referred to it in the fifteenth Canto of his poem *Don Juan*.

All energy was now put into manual work, resulting in more and more material prosperity for the Colony. This worried Rapp who feared that his people might lapse into worldliness. He determined that the only way to avoid this danger was to submit them to more struggle. A move to another location was the only answer to his fears, and he announced that this was necessary because the present location was too far from navigation for marketing their goods. Harmony was put up for sale and realized a good price. Rapp then purchased thirty thousand acres in Posey County, Indiana—watered by the Wabash River.

With ant-like industry the Harmonists dug themselves in again, and in another miraculously short time, they had created a community that was the envy of all other communitarian communities. From their new center they were able to trade with such States as Louisiana and their wares became a great pecuniary success. The fame of the Colony spread far and wide, especially in England, where an eccentric millionaire sociologist was experimenting with communitarian ideas rather unsuccessfully. He crossed the water, went to see Rapp and offered a price for the Colony headquarters that could not be turned down because of its size. The fact that Robert Owen failed in his American communitarian experiment is another testament to Rapp's ability, who always made an unqualified success of his.

And so again the Rappites struck their tents, this time to return to Pennsylvania where they settled on a site near to Pittsburgh, on the banks of the Ohio River. A steamboat was a new acquisition to be used for their own shipping. The new center was called Economy and is to be seen today with several buildings preserved by the State Historical Society. Its name was taken because Rapp now announced that the Colony would embrace the science of economics, deviating somewhat from the former purely agricultural way of life.

Here the Harmonists worked as slavishly as ever. Another model town sprang up as if by magic. Among the new industries Rapp introduced the silkwork, bringing experts from abroad so they could begin making ribbons and velvets, also brocades—all of which became famous in contemporary America. The manufacture of pottery, baskets, and blankets continued to be the main source of income.

Ruled by Rapp's brilliant persuasive powers, the Harmonists continued to live in comparative harmony until an event of seemingly trivial importance grew into such significance that it nearly wrecked the Utopia. It has all the pictorial ingredients of a good moving picture and one day may come to the attention of an enterprising producer of American themes.

A letter came to Rapp one day from a Count Maximilian de Leon who lived at Frankfurt-on-Main in Germany. It was suitably coroneted and was couched in very flattering and reverent language. Rapp was not usually victimized by those who courted his ego, but the inborn snobbery of the German peasant flowed within his veins. Moreover, the Count claimed to be a divine messenger instructed by God Himself that he see all was ready for the arrival of Christ in America. Having experienced a similar mystical incident himself, he could not doubt the truth of this statement. He wrote by return inviting Count de Leon to come and visit the Colony.

Rapp had no way of knowing that de Leon was a complete charlatan, a demon of intrigue and born under a very merry star. He was out to make his fortune by fair means or foul. His arrival at Economy before there had been time for Rapp's invitation to reach him, was merely a symptom of what was going to happen.

Without any warning, he arrived with his suite in a coach-in-four followed by several others. The "Count," complete with sword and three-cornered hat—bearing himself very pompously—was surrounded by uniformed attendants dressed in medieval costume and acted towards him with great servility. It was like a scene from some operetta.

He spoke that night to an eager throng in the Church. What he said was far from being apocalyptic, except that the Millennium was at hand. Rapp sensed that the visit boded no good, but he was unable to prevent the clever way this impostor insinuated his way into the good graces of the Harmonists. He mingled with them artfully, as did his disciples, who were of course rogues, too. The plan was to eventually take over leadership and force Rapp out.

The interlopers preached a seditious doctrine, advocating shorter hours of labor and also proposing that matrimony be reintroduced. All this naturally appealed to the younger Harmonists, of whom a good number were soon adherents of de Leon. Rapp was quick to see that he was dealing with a dangerous charlatan who must be dealt with as such. He saw that if he expelled him and his colleagues by force, he might create a martyrdom. With the astuteness of the fox, he decided to let the bogus Count overplay his hand. He would wait until he could "finesse his enemy's lead."

"Count" de Leon made such headway that one third of the Colony—mostly the younger—decided to secede. Rapp agreed, paid them off and allowed them to form their own group at Posey County, Indiana, the old Harmonist site. As he shrewdly imagined, they did not live long under the aegis of de Leon before he made clear his real purpose. He permitted marriage and much less work—but in return he taxed them a sizable sum each month so that he and his courtiers could live extravagantly at their expense.

After a time they found the "Count" such a luxury they told him they could not afford it. In reply he ordered them to go to Economy and demand, under threat of violence, a greater share of the funds held by Rapp.

A large deputation, suitably armed, obeyed this command and Rapp faced an angry situation for which he had some excellent ammunition of his own. He had caused investigations to be made about de Leon in Germany and he now possessed ample proof of how really bogus he was. After a slight fracas with the disputants, he asked to be heard. With grave simplicity he traced the history of the Harmonists under his own leadership, which truly spoke for itself. Then with lyrical emotion he turned to the schism brought about by de Leon. At his most eloquent he persuaded the crowd that this man was a villain.

The deputation returned to Posey County and drove away the "Count" and his disciples forever. Reunion celebrations followed in the Spring of 1832, but these were accompanied by a tragedy. The loyal adoptive son, Frederick Rapp, died of a heart attack in the midst of it all. This was a great loss because Rapp had always looked upon him as a successor, and he was getting old.

Always an innovator, he now introduced the study of music and painting. An orchestra was formed and concerts were frequent. A Music Hall was built, but as the artists were more in number than the musicians this was used for exhibits, too. Numerical growth of the Colony was hampered by the existing decree of celibacy which, during its brief rescindment by de Leon, had not contributed much towards new birth. Deaths were occurring with monotonous regularity. Ironically, the first oil in the United States was discovered at what is now Titus-

ville, at that time land owned by the Harmonists, opening
a new era and industry for America. The Colony was now
so wealthy that Rapp opened its own Bank, and while cele-
brating all this luck, he suffered a heart attack and died
on August 10, 1847.

With his death, absolute rule ended. Thereafter the
Colony was governed by a Board of Trustees. Without
Rapp's rare personality to make for solidarity, disgruntled
Colonists brought in clever lawyers and disintegration began. By 1850 the Harmonist organization had become
merely a skeleton, lingering on more as a memory than
anything else until 1903, when it was officially disbanded.

At Economy today, the Great House, containing forty-
five rooms and two stories in height, is run as a museum
—preserved by the State Historical Society. It contains
furniture made by the Colonists, also some of the musical
instruments played by the orchestra. The large clock
tower still tolls away the hours as it did for the Harmonists.
Ironically, the Harmonist Church has been taken over by
the Lutherans, the Orthodox Church which Rapp had
come to America to avoid!

Almost all the communitarian communities of the Nineteenth Century ended sometime after the death of the religious zealot who led them. Happily, however, there is a
notable exception that managed to bridge this gap—the
True Inspirationists of Amana, who have had their Colony
in Iowa for over one hundred years.

The sect was founded in Württemberg, Germany, in
1714 as a protest of certain formalities of the existing State
Church. Later, a very remarkable man named Christian
Metz became its inspired prophet. Like Bimeler and Rapp,

he was a marvellous mixture of religion and practicality. He studied Theology, prepared to advance from the ideas it taught to those more in accordance with observed phenomena. He recognized that life was a struggle for existence—and he regarded man as part of Nature—but its noblest part. As such, he felt that man was capable of intellectual and moral progress which was not the mere result of physical laws.

In his native Germany he found his area hopelessly circumscribed. To him there was only one Monarch who rules His world by laws which are flexible in His hands. He dreamed of a benevolent earthly monarchy which could submit to the control of righteousness, of a Christian nobility which would mediate between the crown and the people. To him Society was an organism which grows under providential environment, and revolutions are merely the expiation of sin.

One night in the summer of 1841 he was asleep in his bedroom when there came a knock at the door. He lit a candle, got out of bed, but not a sign of anyone. As the village clock struck the hour of midnight he asked himself if this could have been a supernatural manifestation—but his intellect replied that a disembodied spirit could not knock.

Nevertheless, that part of him which refused to fraternize with reason, would not reject the spiritistic theory. Suddenly he heard the sound of someone murmuring in a corner of his room. He could not distinguish every word but his ears caught the low sounds at the end of every sentence. It sounded like someone teaching a child to say the Lord's Prayer, repeating over and over again sentences taken at random.

Then before his affrightened eyes, there appeared a
Spectre who instructed him to take his flock to a land
where they could practise their beliefs without molesta-
tion. Christian Metz began formulating plans to carry out
this order, which he felt sure came directly from God.

Some of his followers were fairly wealthy men; almost
all owned some special skill. Several hundred Inspirationists sailed for America in the Spring of 1842 to found their
social experiment near Buffalo, at a place they called
Ebenezer. Here they made blankets and woolens of such
quality that a wide reputation was achieved quickly.
Christian Metz ran the Colony brilliantly. Each man did
what he excelled in doing. German was spoken exclusively,
and the Inspirationists introduced methods new to America for agriculture and for pruning trees. They all slept on
the traditional "feather bed," and anyone who died was
buried with an open Bible! Celibacy was not obligatory
but was regarded as the highest spiritual state.

All seemed to be going nicely when Metz had another
mystical experience. This time the portent told him he
must move his Colony to the New Frontier. In the spring
of 1855 they all began the trek Westward, to what was
then Prairie land on the banks of the winding Iowa River.
There he had purchased 18,000 acres, eighteen miles
Southwest of what is now Cedar Rapids—seventy miles
from Davenport.

Here they acquired the village of Homestead. They
built their homes in a rather undistinguished style, all
similar. By 1861, four more villages had been built within
a short distance, all of which still exist. They are known
under their original names: Amana, West Amana, High
Amana, East Amana. Within recent times extensions have

been made, such as at Lower South Amana, where there is a good hotel.

The Colony prospered, manufacturing fine furniture from the cherry and Walnut trees that they grew in abundance. Later Westphaelian hams and cheeses were a speciality which became famous and to this day are sent to all parts of America. Cradles, canopy beds, and Dutch cupboards were sold all over the Commonwealth of Iowa. More German pietists came and joined the Inspirationists who welcomed them in hearty German fashion.

Discipline was strict. Marriage was permitted only if the engaged couple agreed to live in separate villages for one year, after which their parents decided whether they were soul-mates. Dress of both sexes was kept very simple, the female so restricted that the curves of the body not be too pronounced. The Inspirationists loved their gardens, and relieved the simplicity of their homes' exterior by colorful flowers, and vine trellises covering the walls.

A man of commanding presence, Christian Metz continued to be the temporal and spiritual leader until his death in 1867. In his pamphlets, none of which received a wider public than the Colonists, he never attacked existing religions. But he found the disputes between theologians full of curious interest. He honors thought and reason which, he insists, emanates from God, revealing universal and immutable truth. Even if Providence be a mere superstition, he says in effect, why should man not guide his life by good sense and moderation in all things? Had he wished, Metz could undoubtedly have become an influence in American free-thought, but all he wanted was the adoring love of the Amana people, which he bountifully received.

After he died, a Board of Deputies took over from his benevolent rule. This was vested with powers to lessen the spiritual authority, also to allow the infiltration of American ideas. Undoubtedly this Americanization was mainly responsible for the colony succeeding after the death of the leader. Today, the Inspirationists are governed spiritually by the Amana Church Society and temporally by the Amana Cooperative Society, which has fifteen hundred members.

A form of socialized medicine and dole takes care of everyone from cradle to the grave. All enjoy every form of American freedom within the colony—excepting on Sundays, when all forms of pleasure are denied. The young must not use their motor cars, and attendance in Church is the rule. In the old days, the main punishment for pecadilloes was exclusion from Church. Today attendance is still ranked as a privilege not to be missed.

The Inspirationists still manufacture their original lines, making copies of early American furniture for which there is brisk demand. To show how up-to-date they are, a good refrigerator has been added to these products. A visit to the Amanas will show that they are a community of happy and contented men and women who care for the ultimate things of life more than those of vulgar show. If the houses are plain outside, you will find the warmth in the hearts of the present Inspirationists inside the home.

The Father of Washington, D.C.   II. 5

DELIGHT IN THE VISTA HAS ABSORBED ARCHI-
tects abroad for use in designing cities for a very long time;
and perhaps lack of it in the majority of American cities
is one reason for complaint by foreign visitors that they
are too "checkerboard." Who can deny that Washington
is the great exception and is one of the most beautiful in
the world? In no other city, here or abroad, will you see
such lovely converging lines, leading the eye to a point
of rest in the distance. It is, in fact, architecture's crowning contribution to the vista.

Many an appreciative visitor to Washington goes into
raptures over the simultaneous prospect of graceful buildings, tastefully enhanced by Greek columnar relief. They
also comment favorably on the rows of stately trees which
line the avenues, offering the season of the leaf to adorn
the buildings—and winter beauty when boughs are bare.

Much of Washington's charm as a city is due to a
Frenchman who designed the plans for the Federal City
with a prescience that now seems uncanny. He died forgotten, but the renascence of his fame is increasing year
by year. Because he chose deliberately to come to America, where he received posthumous gratitude (as we shall
see), I include him in this book. With such excellent talent,
he would have been widely acclaimed in his own land.

Charles Pierre L'Enfant was born in France in 1755, the son of a competent artist. Early in his life, he discovered his bent for design, and his father had him educated for architecture. At school he came under the influence of the grand schemes that had characterized the building of cities in the times of Louis XIV, a type that has inspired many architects in the use of vast proportions and far-flung perspectives. L'Enfant also studied the landscape designs by such great park and garden architects as Mansard, Le Notre, and Gabriel—which put Washington in his debt.

The time of his arrival in America is disputed. Some say he came with Lafayette, who knew his father; others insist that he arrived aboard one of the ships in the Fleet of Beaumarchais. He served in the early part of the Revolutionary War as a volunteer; then his ability for military architecture came to the notice of General Washington. This led to his appointment as Chief Engineer of the Army, with the rank of Major. He was described at this time as being an erect type of man, six feet tall and owning a handsome face with a rather prominent nose. Some thought him too formal in his manners, also studied in his dress. Often he would wear fancy-frocked shirts, and in cold weather he would be seen in a long, fancy overcoat surmounted by a bell-crowned hat. Observers noted that his voice, clothed in a strong French accent, was authoritarian. In a diary entry, Washington commented that his grammar in speech was much better than what he wrote.

George Washington spoke only fractured French and, never a good speller, always wrote the Major's name as *Lenfang*. He seems to have recognized in L'Enfant from the start a man governed by his conscience rather than self-interest. A little later on he was searching for someone of talent to design a political capital for the new Republic, to be "a State such as had never existed before and which would have no rival." L'Enfant turned out to be the very man.

The Father of his Country had already decided approximately where it would be located. With that vision which was all his own, he chose a site considered today by experts to have been the inevitable. The site of Washington D.C. stood the tactical geographical tests of the Civil War. The choice is even more remarkable when we consider that he made it at a time when the war with England was not yet won and the Republic's continued existence by no means sure. America still had formidable enemies within and without.

Moreover, the location of a federal Capital had to be such that it could not be suspected as belonging to any one State more than another. With the advice of Jefferson, he selected it, therefore, for political rather than aesthetic reasons. Among other things, it had to be near a point of juncture between the Northern and the Southern States— the West then being mainly unexplored territories. The locality of Washington had to be created and neutralized with permission of all the adjoining States for the purpose of placing a Federal Capital within it. Added to all his other services to America, is it any wonder that no memory in this country is as revered as that of George Washington? There is, as is fitting, a comparison of attitude of the Roman Empire to Julius Caesar.

To design such a city must have been the answer to an architect's dream in those far-off days. Imagine the joy

that came to L'Enfant's heart when he was awarded the
high honor of this great work. He could take all the land
he needed within certain limits (a radius was stipulated
of ten square miles). A tract in Maryland and a section
of Virginia were allocated, most of which was free from
dwellings, so he could proceed without the worries of the
average architect today when planning vast projects—
with vested interests such as landlords, civic authorities,
and red-tape routine (not then invented!).

We see him going to survey his demesne. With that
cut of the eye which a true genius usually possesses, he
visualized a Capital which would represent fully the aims
and values of the New World, to him a new universe.
The star would be the Capitol building for which he
chose a hill one hundred feet above the Anacosta and
Potomac Rivers—in fact overlooking the confluence of
both. In constellation, in his mind's eye, he saw what is
now Pennsylvania, New Jersey and Delaware Avenues—
and a number of others which only remained in paper
plans while he lived. The White House he visualized as a
symbolic Satellite which would dominate the lesser important buildings which are essential to an important
Capital.

This choice of a starry heaven he probably borrowed
from France, because it is evident at Versailles and St.
Cloud, from whose centers avenues radiate in all directions. The fact remains that Washington is a center of
beauty and prestige for the American people.

Major L'Enfant was at first given the same freedom of
action enjoyed by the great architects of Versailles, the
Hague of Holland, and Saint Petersberg in Russia—all
Capitals built to order as *bastide* towns. He was given an

area as unobstructed as the sky in which to lay his plans. Obstructionists there were, of course. Thomas Jefferson, then considered the greatest living American architect, wished to see used the right angle for the streets—a design he had made popular in other cities. L'Enfant objected to this system of uniform blocks which chops up a town like a checkerboard with all streets crossing each other— leaving no room for the imagination to take flight.

He persuaded Jefferson that the acute be substituted for his proposed right angle, and he rightly argued that this possessed a military value. These converging streets were of importance when the British attacked the city in 1812, but they are also the secret of much of Washington's great charm in its vistas.

In his plans, L'Enfant also stressed parks and gardens. What is now called the Mall—that open broad Parkway —is actually the Grand Avenue drawn so boldly on his original plans. He envisioned it to stretch from the Capitol grounds to what we now know as Fourteenth Street, and it has since become a keystone of the City's Park system.

It was as if he sensed the need for the tired and worried diplomat to find a place to ponder, somewhere he could identify himself in the familiar surroundings of Nature—a place apart, where the vexations of State would disappear. In this park the European envoy finds endless varieties of trees and plants he knows well abroad, from Spain's Judas tree to the Japanese cherry.

No one seems to have needed such soothing surroundings more than L'Enfant, whose name curiously suggests petulance. In shaping up his plans for the new Federal City, he engaged in a series of quarrels with officialdom. All went well at first, and he received President Washington's sanction for his plans and first drafts. But when the Commissioners requested that he supply prints of them to Members of Congress, to be used in parcelling and selling land of the new city, trouble ensued.

Placing his principles above the value of his job, L'Enfant flatly refused on the ground that illegitimate use might be made of his work. With a certain amount of justice he feared that certain Congressmen would seize the opportunity to indulge in selfish speculation, which would result in disfigurement of his dream city. For this disobedience he was summarily dismissed.

Through intrigue from his enemies, his friendship with Washington ended in estrangement, but as a secret gesture the President was instrumental in having him appointed the designer of a new project, the manufacturing town of Paterson, New Jersey. L'Enfant worked on the plans, as the right angle streets there would indicate— but again his temperament got the better of him and he was dismissed after a few months.

Meanwhile, illegitimate use of his plans for Washington, D.C. was made, as he had feared, because he had overlooked the necessity of copyrighting them. Unfairly his fee for them was withheld for eighteen years, which came just in time to see him through the last year of his life. This was in 1825, when he received the sum of $1394.63, being the amount of his fee plus eighteen years interest. Irrational to the very end, he died boarding with some friends in Prince George County, Maryland. It is said he died clasping a copy of his precious plans to his heart.

By the end of the nineteenth century Washington's insight, and L'Enfant's foresight for the city, were proven correct. The growth of Washington, D.C. was slow but constant, and it has gradually emerged as a fitting Capital for a wealthy and proud nation—modelled, as both men had wished, for a new era and epoch of history.

The White House was built on the exact site suggested by L'Enfant for what was first called the President's House. The cornerstone for it was laid by George Washington himself in 1792. He lived long enough to walk through the building when it was near completion, but he never resided there.

Up until 1814 it was called the President's House, and not many people seem to know why the name was changed. This was due to the Irish architect who designed the building, James Hoban of County Kilkenny, hunted out of Ireland by the British for Fenian activity. After the British sacked Washington in the War begun in 1812, it was black with gunsmoke. Renovation was needed and James Hoban was engaged to do the work. He ended by painting the house white to cover the ugly scars of war, hence the change in name.

Which reminds me of the tale they tell of a sedate English lady, who never had come to America and was the type that never would. When told that her countrymen burned Washington, she exclaimed: "I am aware that our Army were forced to execute a number of American rebels, but I never heard before that we had martyred an American President!"

To return to L'Enfant, his end was possibly a happy one. If, as some believe, the dead can look down and observe what goes on among the living, he was happy at last. In 1902 President Taft ordered that his remains be brought from oblivion and reinterred with full military honors at Arlington Cemetery where they now repose.

On a sunny spring day of that year, Mr. Elihu Root, then
Secretary of State, presided at the ceremony and said:
"Few men can afford to wait one hundred years for
recognition. It is not a change in L'Enfant that brings us
here. We have to confess that it is we ourselves who have
changed and are now better able to appreciate his genius . . ."

President Taft sent a message admitting roundly that
the original plans of Major L'Enfant had stood the test
of a century, also they had met with universal approval.
Departure from them had always been regretted and
wherever possible would now be remedied.

But in praising this little-known nephew of Uncle Sam,
let us also admit that the improvements since President
Taft sent his message have approached even further what
L'Enfant wished to make of Washington, D.C. He can
say what Wren said about London: "If you would see my
work, just look around you."

SEVEN? THERE ARE MORE LIKE SEVENTY-
seven! The question is mainly one of taste and choice.
For the Speoleologist, there are the ice caves of Mount
Rainier, or those of Mammoth in Kentucky—which have
never been fully explored. Those who like mystery should
visit the fossil footprints in the sandstone quarries near
Carson City, Nevada. A Paleontologist's paradise will be
found in the bone quarries of Wyoming where there is
embedded the richest store of prehistoric remains in the
world. Antiquity lovers must see the giant earthen structure built by the Indians in Ohio two thousand years ago;
or the Petrified Forest of Arizona, a vegetation of solid
stone due to a mystifying mineralization.

Americans who have studied the lives of Washington,
Jefferson, Lincoln, and "Teddy" Roosevelt should not fail
sometime to go to Mount Rushmore, where their images
are carved out of the mountainside of basalt rock. While
the acclaim that the world gives to these great American
Presidents can never be ours, the sight of this wonder can
help us in the cultivation of their courage and sympathies.

Lesser wonders are galore: the Blue Canyon of Colorado
offers a riot of colors; and the Enchanted Mesa of New
Mexico awaits the seeker after desert beauty. Lovers of

history should not miss the "American Thermopylae," the historic ruins of a Chapel and Monastery, where heroes fought and died at San Antonio. And as an example of a true American oddity, there is to be seen at Eureka Springs the only Church in the world which you must enter through the steeple. This is in the heart of the mystical Arkansas Ozark Mountains, which are worth a book in themselves.

In choosing what I feel are America's seven best wonders, I am treating on mainly the great sights of nature. You do not have to have poetic vision—to see the world in a grain of sand or heaven in a wild flower—to thoroughly enjoy these sights. You only have to use your eyes, but we have to learn to look before we know fully how to see. In order to appreciate these sights better, don't fail to read what experts have to say before you pay them a visit. My own impressions of them are set down fully aware that better writers have seen them with sharper eyes than myself.

By thus increasing the pleasure of observation you enjoy all the more the pleasure of reflection, which should always be more of a delight than the actual moment. Don't forget that sounds and scents belong essentially to the particular scene you behold. Never let your eyes be lazy. Exert and train them until they regard all the startling and conflicting detail in the scene you are observing. If you put the surrounding objects in suitable relation to each other, the immediate world around you will become a picture.

Lastly, it should never be forgotten what we owe to our National Park System, which is run by and for dedicated Americans, who believe that for them to understand the beauties of the land is to have faith in her future. Because of them we still have huge pieces of beauty, while other countries are losing theirs and blaming it on progress.

THE GRAND CANYON
(First Wonder)

Niagara Falls and the Grand Canyon may be said to be the only American phenomena on which all foreign critics agree to lavish praise. No one can deny that the Grand Canyon is the most astounding piece of natural architecture in the world, nor that, with hundreds of pretentious rivals, Niagara Falls is the monarch of them all.

A perfect description of the Canyon would bankrupt the English language and might result in just a flood of adjectives, if only because there is nothing by way of comparison. Some observers have likened it to the Himalayas and in the grandeur of color there is comparison. It is in fact the riot of colors with which you must first come to terms, the flaming reds and crimsons—softened a little by the chocolate-browns and blue-greens. Slowly it dawns upon you that here are colors, like the plunging green of Niagara, which cannot be portrayed on any canvas. The mixture is a secret of God Himself.

The Canyon's vast dimensions at first overwhelm one, but gradually the chaotic immensity takes on harmonious form as one realizes that here is architecture which no generation of men could copy satisfactorily. Here one becomes aware of the Creator who promises eternal life;

here is a perfect place for worshipping the Divine Intelligence, which seems everpresent.

To the geologic student, the Canyon unfolds in its sides all the strata from the Carboniferous period down to that of Archaean Granite. The way to see this is to take the trip to the floor, a descent into another world. View follows view as one passes through several climatic zones in a six thousand feet decline. Those prehistoric "villages" and turret-crowned "castles" take on a different aspect from the one they gave above, where they lack relief. Down below those Egyptian, Roman, and Greek "Temples" loom up sharply against the sky.

At every turn there is some vista that cries out for remembrance. As you descend, the Colorado River, merely a narrow thread seen from above, takes on larger and larger proportions. The nearer you come you hear the gentle roar more and more forcibly, as it continues to cut its canyon as it has been doing for millenniums. Soon you see it is really a furious muddy flood, lashing its way between steep walls of granite. What a contrast to the silvery filament seen from the rim above.

The distance to the floor is only six miles, but the return journey seems like double—all uphill. Like all things that are immense, the Canyon tests one in several ways, even at times to the point of seeming unfriendly. Like every steel-true personality it wants to know you better before admission to its circle. By the time you have returned to the surface, you have learned to know this sublime spectacle as a distinct architectual whole, an organized Cosmos. The colors no longer daze you; the palisades now smile instead of giving off that forbidding frown. You have made a friend whom you vow to see again.

NIAGARA FALLS
(Second Wonder)

An American lecturer was lately talking about the Great Cataract to an audience of potential tourists to America in England. He showed a slide of Goat Island, whereupon a deaf English dowager said: "I always knew that Rhode Island was one of the smaller States, but I didn't know it was as small as that!"

Goat Island is, of course, the least important attraction of Niagara Falls. To really become acquainted with the Falls, you should visit the Cave of the Winds, which necessitates walking along a ridge beneath Goat Island. In order to do this, you step down some stairs which cling to the face of the cliff. Rounding a sharp corner, the Falls greet you, sweeping from the height above with a deafening roar and a blinding spume. You feel the fretting spray on your face!

Now you climb some huge rocks, linked by bridges and leading to the face of Niagara herself. You pass right in front of the torrents gliding over the precipice with effortless ease. Seemingly they break at your feet in clouds of spray, beating with a hoarse roar upon the gorge.

You descend some more steps at the base of a large rock, which is like a small beachhead lashed by a sea of waves, and here is the Cave, from which you cannot turn back. It is a nightmare of wind all right, and you wish somehow that the crashing water would stop so you could comment to your companion. But it suddenly dawns upon you that Niagara never stops, save when it is festooned with icicles in winter.

The Cave of the Winds is really not a cave at all, but what it lacks in name it makes up in wind. For it is really only a pathway suitably railed off under the base of the precipice from which the American Falls fling themselves. Descending in so great a gush, they are naturally thrown forward from the rock's face, leaving a passage for you to walk beneath.

To get the best view of Niagara in its truest tumult, the American side has it. There you see this universe of water—miles and tons of it—roaring with irresistible speed and force over the abyss. Scientists say that it took thirty-five thousand years for the river to gnaw through the corraline stone in order to change its course for its present precipitation over the Horseshoe Falls. From the American side the river runs into Goat Island, where half of it leaps aside and turns the Canadian corner.

The stream of rapids is fascinating to watch as it curls into an arc of the most wondrous green, a shade that could never reach an artist's palette correctly. Then it becomes just huge white walls of water accompanied by floating clouds of spray, which reach the bottom a trifle weary after such buffeting—turning to a sluggish green below.

If you return to the Falls at Sunset, you may see the famous rainbow—and should you be sufficiently superstitious you may see Wenonah and Uncas, the phantom lovers, sacrificing their youthful lives over the Falls to save their tribe from famine.

Wenonah is said to come first, blindly sailing over the rapids, rushing towards the brink in her traditional white canoe. Uncas, her betrothed, unable to bear the separation, dashes for his own canoe and follows his beloved to the

death. As they disappeared, a lovely rainbow formed and
it is within these colors that the legend is spectrally re-
enacted—and witnessed many times by those gifted with
second-sight!

THE GARDEN OF THE GODS
(Third Wonder)

Not far from Denver two enormous portals of red sandstone flash greetings to you, framing Pike's Peak against
a Colorado sky of blue. Here, where it would seem that
a god has gone delightfully mad, are fantastic examples
of natural phenomena—colored sandstone rocks capri-
ciously sculptured by wind and rain, both helped by
atmospheric gasses.

Placed in macabre disorder over a vast acreage are
almost perfect images of dolphins and griffins—some with
the legs of a lion, others pointing the beak of an eagle.
There are weird groupings of birds of prey ready to
pounce, or snarling beasts, prehistoric in appearance—
all motionless and silent, frozen into stone. As you travel
about, grotesque gargoyles appear unexpectedly from
some outcropping of rock, such as those decorating the
exterior of an ancient Cathedral or the cornices of a ruined
Pagan temple.

There is a feeling of being in an Alice-in-Wonderland
world as you witness what must be Nature's greatest
practical joke. Towering toadstools, mindful of Aesop's
Fables, appear to the right and left, tall enough for a
grown man to stand beneath. Thickly strewn among these
are every imaginable size and shape of rock, so super-

natural in design as to suggest the climax of some terrific convulsion of Nature.

Here is the Balancing Rock, a vast cubical boulder of red sandstone which has tottered there since time immemorial. It has been likened to the Rocking Pagoda in Burma, and there is a resemblance even if this great mass of stone has no temple built on it. Other pieces of phenomenal erosion have been given such arresting names as the Statue of Liberty and Cathedral Spire, although they hint more accurately at ruins of vast Aztec temples or shrines of ancient gods. Two more striking examples of erosion called the Siamese Twins are topped with ogre-like heads fixed with bulbous eyes and rude protruding lips, a little suggestive of Victor Hugo's Hunchback of Notre Dame.

Presiding over this curious collection of fantastica is Pike's Peak (named after Zebulon Pike), with its lovely enclosed valleys and cloud-patched plains and parks. Up there you'll get a splendid view of the Holy Cross, immortalized by Longfellow—the symbol of American hope.

YELLOWSTONE PARK
(Fourth Wonder)

Someone has said that the geysers of Yellowstone are like a mighty open-air kitchen where the cooks have forgotten their pots. They are, of course, constantly overboiling. In one of these, situated in the Yellowstone Lake itself, you may cook your fish in the boiling hot spring after catching it in the cold fresh-water surrounding!

The Snow Mountains, born of volcanic action, lift their lofty heads around you in this already well-elevated

Valley. The Park, teeming with geysers, mud-springs, valleys, canyons and even a natural bridge, is a plateau fifty-five miles long by sixty-five miles wide—so there is much to see in it. There are also numerous wild gorges, lakes and dancing cascades. Small wonder that it is a mecca for tourists each summer, who come mainly to see the geysers.

Interestingly enough, not all the geysers are old. Artemesia Geyser only came into action in 1886, which is very recent as geysers seem to measure time. And, contrary to rumor, not all of them behave according to rule. Excelsior (meaning the highest) ruptured its lungs in 1888 and has never been the same since. Old Faithful, named by the first white man whom it welcomed to the plateau, is sometimes known as Guardian of the Valley and is still the most obedient geyser for its uniform periodicity of action. Nevertheless, Giant Crater still holds the record for making the most explosive noises.

My favorite part of Yellowstone is at Paint Pot Basin, the name of which describes it very well. Scattered with customary prodigality are large and small pots of purling, bubbling mud looking as smooth and fresh as manufactured paint of every imaginable hue—white, orange, green, violet, blue and brown. Clots of this colorful excrescence are banked up around the craters. A companion group of paint pots nearby exudes ferric acid in such abundance that the scene is red with blood, a good representation of Dante's grand word picture of the rivers of fire in Hades! All this brilliantly colored mud hisses and bubbles, continually making a weird commotion as one bubble after another bursts explosively.

On a guided tour you are taken from spring to spring,

geyser to geyser, where boiling hot water pulsates in steaming waves overflowing its basin. Many of these have exquisitely fretted rims varying in color with a touch of Nature, which no human hand could imitate. Here and there are stalagmites, shining iridescently at their edges in shades of red, brown, green and yellow.

Beauty there is on every side, the wild beauty of untamed nature—lofty mountains dominating the scene. Yellowstone is one of Nature's masterpieces, and is an experience at once of terror, wonder, and delight. My only criticism is that it is not appropriately named. It ought to be rechristened *Aqua Caliente,* which means *Hot Water.* That is probably what the Spanish would have called it had they been the first discoverers.

CRATER LAKE
(Fifth Wonder)

The most perfect mirror lake in the world exists in the Cascade Mountains in Oregon and is far more impressive than the crater lakes of Southern Germany. The Indians called this one "Spirit Lake" because they found immediate repose in its presence.

By rights, only those who pass muster with the Recording Angel deserve to go there, yet mere average mortals are allowed to go there—proving once again that America gives us more than our deserts. You and you and you may revel in that peace that passes all understanding at Crater Lake. She rests there aloof to the world, and one can picture the Pagan Indians in their solitary devotions here.

The secret of the Lake's beauty is in the unique en-

closure of its chalice. No breeze ever ruffles its surface
because the water lies nearly one thousand feet below
its precipitous rim, which is twenty miles in circumference.
This gives an amazing perspective to the compression of
the scene, offering all, as it were, in one cut of the eye—
the crater walls acting as an embracing whole. This combines to provide the visitor with a peculiar glory, a
fascination that can only be hinted at in words.

An island rises out of the southern portion of the lake—
a volcanic cone within the crater. It reminds me strongly
of Saint's Island in Lough Derg, County Donegal, on
which Davoc, the follower of St. Patrick, founded a
monastery which has ever since been a pilgrimage for the
devout. So I am going to suggest that the island within
Crater Lake was used for certain secret rites in the days
when it was only known to the Indians! Here is the perfect setting for the pantheistic mystic.

In the crater orifice, as in the walls of the Grand Canyon, you have the whole story of geology, for those who
like that subject. There are to be seen the various stages
of the earth's beginnings delineated in detail by the
glacial and volcanic fabrics. Strong evidences of the
Ice Age can be seen here and there, with markings of
eskers, moraines, and "strirae."

Towering above the reflective waters are Glacier Peak
and Kerr Notch which can be seen mirrored below the
charming walks that border the crater. Go to one of the
rims and peer down over a ledge. What a scene for the
memory storehouse! Photograph it in your mind for
future recollection. No camera can do it justice, nor can
an artist capture it perfectly. He who has not set eyes on
this picture does not know the true beauty of America.

THE AMERICAN ACROPOLIS
(Sixth Wonder)

Rising out of the center of a magical valley containing natural bridges, mushroom erosions, and bastions of many shapes, is the oldest and oddest city in America—the Acoma Pueblo. It sits there on the elevation of its mesa, seemingly dead but with life in every lovely line. It is a place to forget time, to be at peace. Those who fashioned her put something of sublimity into this haven that cannot be easily described.

Acoma is invested with weird, irresistible power which seizes the imagination. Ghosts peer out of the dwellings, whose walls are ready to whisper her story to willing ears. She stands there on a great table rock nearly four hundred feet high in this lovely setting, which is already an altitude of seven thousand feet. To reach this lofty eyrie you only have to travel sixty miles west of Albuquerque, then on foot to its summit by a track between crags and boulders.

Every part of the fortress rock is haunted by antiquity and romance. It was ancient when the Spaniards came in 1540 and has been continually inhabited except for a brief period when it was sacked after an altercation with Spanish rule. Sixteen priests were stoned to death by the Indians and a massacre took place in 1599, when they trapped and killed a party of Spanish soldiers. In retaliation for this outrage the city was wrecked and the Indians were forced to camp elsewhere until they could lovingly restore it.

Since then they have lived their unmolested, largely because the soil is not very productive and no one has coveted it. They indulge in dry farming, much the same as their ancestors—growing melons, pumpkins and corn with a water supply accumulated from melted snow and cloud bursts in summer.

Life propels round the Square. These Pueblo Indians are essentially agricultural. They are men of grave demeanor, taciturn yet dignified—but not morose or unkindly. It is unlikely that you will hear them use expletives of blasphemy when little things go wrong. Significantly, there are none in any Indian dialect, so they have to use recourse to ours should they feel the need to swear.

The Amerinds of Acoma take great pride in showing tourists their Sky City. They show little or no interest in the outside world, and their own life of harshness and precariousness appeals to them deeply. What they have seen or heard of modern civilization, they are inclined to mistrust it.

Their Pueblo dwellings are three stories high and designed on a clever graduating scale. The rooms are three deep on the ground floor, two on the first, one on the second—so that the roofs of the lower floors provide pleasant promenades.

Behind the Mission Church (1629) there is an extensive cemetery laid out with as much loving care as the Church itself, which has been lately restored. Roman Catholicism must have taken a long time to convert them from their Pagan worship, for it was deeply ingrained in them. These children of the sky revered the sky because on its proper function depended their health and wealth, such as it was. Their Sky Religion was really one of fertility, praying for increase of progeny and crops—very similar to that which the ancient Egyptians worshipped.

Acoma is a travel book in itself, and one of the wonders of the Southwest. Other American cities will go on altering beyond recognition, but Acoma will always be the same —unchanged and unchanging.

THE HUMAN SWALLOWS
(Seventh Wonder)

Les Eyziés, near Perigeux in Southern France, sprang to fame in 1862 when important discoveries of Stone Age and Neanderthalic Man were made. Since then archaeologists and anthropologists have come from far and wide to dig for more evidence, carefully supervised by the French Government. I visited Les Eyziés not long ago, inspected the caves of my ancestors—their chipped flints and bone-carvings. I also saw some fine examples of their art adorning the walls.

Sometime later I heard of the prehistoric cliff-dwellings and cave habitations of the Aboriginal Americans in our Southwest. I soon found that there is far more to be appreciated here than at Les Eyziés, and for those who think that America does not possess antiquity, a tour of this district should make them wax modest about Dynastic Egypt or Persepolis. If these ruins were anywhere else but the U.S.A. tourist companies would organize excursions to see them on a very large scale. I wonder why this is so?

For a long time it seemed as if the knowledge of the early inhabitants of this Continent would remain hidden unless and until Occult science would lift the veil. Now, thanks to deep and efficient research by American archaeologists, it is known that human life has existed here for at least 35,000 years. It is now generally recognized that the aboriginal American's beliefs and customs resembled those in other remote parts of the world.

Much startling and fascinating information has been revealed in the last few years about the culture and movements of a mysterious people who attained a fair degree of civilization and make the arrival of Columbus to this hemisphere less important than we think. The prehistoric cave dwellings such as may be seen at Kajarito Park in the Jemez Plateau of New Mexico, date back ten thousand years or more. They were made in volcanic cones, with entrances into which you have to drop through a hole, the chamber of which is not as uncomfortable as it may sound.

These cones are literally honeycombed with former habitations, resembling gigantic bee-hives. The rock is soft, the result of much erosion, so that the Indians found the caves easy to adapt for living purposes. Inside, the walls were found to have been plastered with mud to make them more home-like. There can be seen ideographic writing on some bare walls of some caves that proves these people had their own sign-language. They were very adept at basket-making.

The Shrine of Makatch, near the Painted Cave of Rio de los Frijoles, appears to have been a sun-worshipping temple, and for these people the sun was, of course, father of all. The entrance is guarded by two lions in crouching position, and the shrine itself is enclosed by a surround of great standing stones, often called the "Stonehenge of America."

There are numberless ruined settlements throughout the Rio Grande country, a few occupied by a mysterious race now called the "Cliff-dwellers." These Amerinds built, where possible, under overhanging cliffs for the sake of greater protection from marauding tribes. The layers of shale alternating with sandstone in this region were particularly adapted for the needs of these human swallows, who built all their "cities" within the protecting crevices.

The Cliff-dwellers were also fortunate because the soil is rich in peroxide of iron, making for a hard mud to be used as cement. This is also a major factor in having preserved their ruins. The adobes still stand wholly in some instances due to the knowledge of stresses and strains these people used in building them, implying a knowledge of rudimentary Geometry.

Mesa Verde (Green Table) National Park may be entered from U.S. 160, midway between Cortez and Mancos in Colorado. This is where the finest ruins of the Cliff-dwellers may be seen. The "city" now known as Cliff Palace, was only discovered in 1888, accidentally, when two ranchers were scouting for some lost cattle. It contains about two hundred living rooms, twenty-three kivas, and numerous other smaller rooms. The tallest tower is four stories in height, and in places there are eight floor levels.

Archaeologists who came to see the ruins were especially struck by a sun-worshipping temple, which one of them was quick to note had never been completed. This Temple had been erected to a revered god, and it must have been left unfinished for good reason. It was clear that here had lived a race of aboriginals who had attained a higher culture than any other. They had learned something about the aesthetics of architecture, also had built into their walls fireplaces with flues. Houses were constructed of specially shaped rocks fixed in adobe mortar. Artistic designs in various colors gave the finishing touch, and pottery as graceful as any from ancient Egypt has been discovered.

Here aboriginal Americans had loved, labored, fought and lost; here they had enjoyed family life, the peace of home much as Americans know it today. In simple obedience to Nature, life was probably joyously welcomed and death accepted by an uncomplaining stoicism. Who were these mysterious people, where did they come from? What happened that made them leave the place they must have loved? What scenes of the past could be evoked if, by means of a magic device, the past could be recaptured on these walls. What drama would be unfolded!

It seemed as if the origin and mystery of these Americans would become as much of a riddle as the Mayans of Yucatan. Then attempts were made to gauge an approximate date of origin of the cliff-dwellings by comparing the timber used with the cross-sections of living trees. This was in excellent preservation due to the dry Colorado air, and guesses were hazarded.

Not very long ago, Professor A. E. Douglass of the University of Arizona, developed a new technique of matching the tree rings in which he was able to assay not only age but also climatic conditions in ancient times. This fixed with a good degree of certainty that some of the cliff-dwellings date back to about the first quarter of the Christian era, and it also proved that about the year 1275 a terrible drought began which drove the cliff-dwellers elsewhere. They had been conquered, but not by marauding tribesmen, as some archaeologists had imagined.

Spruce Tree House, at Mesa Verde Park, offers a feeling of lush contentment somewhat alien to the other ruins. It was built in the cleft of a cliff suggestive of the way mud-swallows make their nests. It contains one hundred and fourteen living rooms and eight ceremonial halls, used in their day for initiation or social purposes. Until about 1880 this was perhaps the largest apartment building in U.S.A.! Opposite is the farming section where formerly melons and corn were grown—those crops which failed in the lean harvest which defeated these mysterious people.

Montezuma's Castle and Well are about five miles from Camp Verde and well reward a visit. Built as a nest of thirty rooms of four stories, the swallows omitted chimneys, and you may still see the smoke-marked walls just as they left them on that fateful day everyone left, never to return.

The ruins of Mesa Verde hold a prominent position in the history of vanished races. There are no more cliff-dwellers there, and we may well ask ourselves if we ourselves are now the real cliff-dwellers—we who live in large cities and inhabit cliff-like apartment houses!

The Great Northwest   III. 2

A RECENT PIECE OF LITERARY TREASURE-trove—some letters written by Jonathan Swift—reveal that he had been reading books by Dampier and de Fucas when his *Gulliver's Travels* was well advanced in MS. Significantly both these famed explorers had penetrated as far as our Northwest in their Seventeenth Century explorations. Swift mentions in a letter that he was especially impressed with *Parchas: His Pilgrimes*, by de Fucas—after whom the Straits are named (but by whom they were not discovered).

Scholars are now certain that the great Irish author drew heavily from this book for the background wherein he set some of the amazing adventures of Lemeul Gulliver. And what probably caught the fancy of Swift was de Fucas describing so alarmingly what is now called Destruction Island, that bleak rock of huge proportions which is still considered the worst risk to shipping on that remote part of the Northwest.

Another description, which he adapted, concerned the two rocky islets which guard the mouth of the Quillayate River at LaPush in the most Northerly part of Washington State. They are weird in shape and have become known as the Drinking Elephants because of their striking resemblance to those large animals.

It was on these rocks, in the mind's eye of Swift, that the stupid page set down Gulliver's box. Just as he saw the surf beating with almost supernatural effect for the Flanflasnic of his Gulliver, you may see it beating today against these islets. There you may view the Olympics "rising sheer on all sides of the Peninsula" as culled by Swift from de Fuca's description and exaggerated by him to be thirty miles high. He called them the Brobdingnagians, peopled them with the giants discovered by Gulliver. The books by Dampier and de Fuca chimed beautifully with the imagination of Jonathan Swift, who had the power of enforcing momentous truth by ludicrous representation. But what he did not know was that these writers he used for embellishing his own concept for the land of Gulliver had already embroidered it with their own exaggerated dimensions. However, was Swift wrong in his? With truly prophetic vision he told of large cities, now a reality. He envisioned the wilderness of the Northwest as being very mountainous, which was found to be true by those who later penetrated it. All this he described in the first edition of *Gulliver*, which was published anonymously in 1726, under the title *Travels into Several Remote Nations of the World.*

In visiting Mount Tacoma we may bring to it all the more interest by thinking of Swift's inner vision enshrined in his immortal book. It was named after Rainier, the explorer, and has since been rechristened Mount Tacoma —but it answers to both names. You reach it by travelling about fifty miles from Tacoma City. A solitary snowclad volcanic peak, it gently slopes for about five thousand feet—then sharply rises to a total of nearly fifteen. The circumference of its base is nearly forty miles.

The companion Mounts Baker, Hood, and St. Helena are all good distances apart. In this the Cascade Range is considered superior to any in Switzerland for the way this isolation accentuates the regiment formation; whereas the Swiss peaks are all jumbled together. Nor do those of Switzerland possess the dark forest bases and low-lying hills, contrasting with the snowy beauty and making them like pieces of frozen music.

To see these Queens at best advantage on a clear day, it is better to travel onto the South shore of the de Fuca Straits, where the Olympics stand out in review like royalty, with Tacoma and Baker in splendid isolation. All around are stretches of fertile lands, smiling valleys covered with timber. The region has much heavier rainfall than California, which perhaps accounts for a larger number of fur-bearing animals. The country has many grizzly bears, panthers, and several kinds of deer.

The view of all views is to be seen from Tacoma's summit. There, in all their glory, are the forests, rivers, emerald valleys—and far away the spires and roofs of growing cities. Look seawards and Puget Sound offers scenes of unsurpassed grandeur. Unless it be the view from Mount Shasta in California, I can think of no more lovely line than these mountains cutting the horizon on a summer evening. There is something inexpressibly appealing as the eye ranges in all directions and the vision of lesser peaks becomes bolder, especially those formed by the terrific upheaval in the glacial period. Tacoma City's harbor is clearly outlined, crowded with ships bound for the Orient, which is three hundred miles nearer to Canton, and other Chinese Ports, than sailing from San Francisco.

Appropriately Puget Sound is called the "Mediterranean of the Pacific" because of the way the sea is continually coquetting with the shore. From above you can see what an important indentation it is. Habitations of all kinds crowd its foreshore or climb its surrounding hillsides. A hum of human activity resounds when one visits it in person, and only then can one appreciate the immense amount of commerce that clusters round it.

Puget Sound must be travelled to be fully enjoyed. It is a sheet of water without equal anywhere, with fifteen hundred miles of irregular tide water-line—all without shoals and fringed with fir, cedar and spruce trees. It is really a system of fjords, dotted here and there with islands that form a splendid feature of the topography.

Ships can anchor anywhere in perfect safety. Fish of all

kinds abound such as smelt, halibut, cod, sturgeon, the latter of which sometimes weighs up to one thousand pounds. Fishermen come here from other lands and ask themselves if they have ever really fished before!

THE MOTHER RIVER

With its magnificent background of eternally snowclad mountains of truly mighty form, the Columbia River claims rightfully to own the greatest river scenery in the world. Of all rivers it is the fifth largest, and the only one that penetrates the Cascades.

Its source is from Columbia Lake, in a part of Canada that is Southeast of British Columbia. In its winding journey it goes North through the Rockies, then South to the State of Washington. In its Western course it divides the State from the border of Oregon, and after approaching the Sierras it breaks through the highlands crowned by Mount Hood, continues North passing Mount Adams and St. Helena.

With a certain amount of justice, the Columbia has been called the "Mother of the Northwest"; and no trip to this region is complete without a tour of its beauties, acclaimed by some observers as superior to the St. Lawrence, the Danube, the Rhine, or the Elb.

An interesting curiosity of this titanic waterway is about one hundred miles East of Portland. It is an island known locally as Cemetery Isle, which looks more like an anchored barge. But what resembles the funnel of the barge is actually the grave-marker of the only body now interred there.

Cemetery Island was originally used as a burial site by

the Indians a couple of thousand years ago. Here in noble splendor they laid their dead, and their philosophy so attracted a man named Victor Treavitt that he ordered his remains to be sent there in 1883. Far from confronting the Great Reaper with repulsion, they courted his companionship! To remind them that life is fleeting and that it is wise to make the most of every passing hour, they wore a small skeleton symbol of the human form which was always interred with them.

Mr. Treavitt wanted to be on the same good terms with death when it struck him. He stated in his last Will that he wished to be buried with the Memaloose Indians, who were "honester than any white man I have known and faced death in a way I like. I will take my chances in the Resurrection with these braves."

However, sometime in the middle of the last Century, the bones of the Indians were removed because it was feared that the island might be washed away by the floodgates of the nearby Bonneville Dam. Accordingly they were reinterred on the mainland in consecrated ground. But when the authorities tried to remove the remains of Victor Treavitt, legal difficulties supervened. He had paid for his plot of land and further instructions in his Will emphatically declared that his body was not to be removed under any circumstances. It has not been washed away yet, and let us hope his soul has gone to the Arcadia of the Indian braves he so admired.

A trip on the Columbia River gives one a fine opportunity to study the beauties of queenly Mount Hood. Mount Shasta can be seen at certain distances silhouetted proudly in Northern California, although it seemingly belongs to Oregon. Half its slope is evergreen and the higher part clad in lasting ermine. Its glaciers feed hundreds of streams which thread this region in all directions and feed another great river, the Sacramento.

All along this incredible waterway there are tumbling creeks and glorious cataracts against a background of sparkling bright-green mosses. All these have their own charming names, such as Shepherd's Dell and Latourelle —two names that alone would inspire a good poet to versify. Another large creek, called the Gorge, is famous for its waterfalling height, musically trickling from the Palisades above onto which Mount Hood supplies much melted snow from her ravines.

The Story of Blind Tom   III. 3

IN STUDYING AMERICA, I HAVE NOTICED THAT —as in Ireland—it is often the unpredictable, not the inevitable, that occurs. Anyone who cares to do some research will find that for every instance of bad treatment of slaves in the Old South, there were one hundred of kindness and fosterage—not that I am defending slavery in any way. Here is a story illustrating this side of a sad part of American history, which proves, however, that some slaves had advantages over their free brothers in Africa. It is an amazing story and could only have happened in America.

A man named General Bethune, who disliked slavery

as much as Abraham Lincoln, was a benevolent Southern gentleman of Columbus, Georgia. He was wealthy enough to indulge in the philanthropic enterprise of buying slaves to send them to the North, where he would secure suitable jobs for them. On one occasion he bought a Negro woman at Muscogee (not far from his home), the mother of several children. One of these had been born blind and was thrown in at no extra charge. According to his custom, the General offered to free her and her children, but the woman flatly refused. As if clairvoyant, she decided to put herself and her blind child in the hands of this noble gentleman—through whom her pathetic baby would grow up to become world-famous.

Blind Tom, as he was nicknamed at birth, was born in 1849 and was about eighteen months old when purchased. A doctor had declared that he was not only incurably blind, but also mentally defective because his nervous reflexes were not normal. His eyes possessed no retina or iris, a congenital deformity—but this freak of Nature was to turn out to be as wonderful, in his own way, as the Natural Bridge of Virginia.

General Bethune had three daughters, all in their teens, who took a great fancy to the pickaninny. After a while they allowed him the run of the house, and he toddled about everywhere. He listened very attentively when the girls sang him lullabyes. To their astonishment one day they stood transfixed as he sang back in perfect pitch what they sang. When he was one year older, he suffered an attack of whooping cough which left him with a husky but not unpleasing tone of voice—totally unlike that of a child. His singing faculty quickly developed and he demonstrated a very remarkable accuracy of ear.

Tom never cared for the company of other children, always preferring to play by himself in games of his own invention. He spent hours staring at the sun with his white, inanimate eyes. Or he would hide himself for the whole day, high up in an old oak tree in the hinterland of the Bethune plantation.

Just before he reached the age of four, the General bought a piano for his daughters. Tom heard the young ladies playing ditties on it, and one day worked up enough courage to try his own prowess on the new instrument. It happened to be raining outside and the Bethune girls sat transfixed as he interpreted beautifully the sound of wind and rain, even to the noise of the water falling onto the gutters. His little fingers picked out the notes perfectly to do this.

As time went on he listened to more classical pieces which the girls played, and he was always able to render perfectly what he had heard. Then one day the General took him to the local Church where he was shown an organ for the first time. After hearing Bach's Fugue 17, he sat at the instrument and played it back as perfectly as everyone present had heard it.

A German piano teacher was suggested, but when the man came to give Tom his first lesson in musical theory, Tom wasn't interested. No matter how hard he tried, the boy could not master the thirty-two bar pattern, nor could he grasp the fact that each note has an exact and unchangeable relationship with all others. Tom only needed to listen to music being played and he could repeat it impeccably. Finally the teacher gave up. "This child knows more music than I could ever learn if I live to be one hundred!" he sighed.

At the age of eight he could stretch an octave, which increased his great musical gifts. Soon his foster-father took him concertizing in the Southern cities, where he created a very great sensation. During a stop for a performance at Washington, he was taken to visit the United States Senate. Tom listened to some of the leading orators of the time and to the utter confounding of a few, he repeated in perfect tone of voice and accuracy of word what some of them had said. At least one of the Senators was glad to see the back of Blind Tom!

As the child-prodigy's fame increased invitations came from Europe to arrange for his appearance over there. This was in 1861 when Tom was twelve years old, and he remained abroad concertizing all of the Civil War years —the faithful General Bethune always by his side. In Berlin Tom was heard by Franz Liszt who reluctantly admitted that he was a genius because he played the Maestro's music as well as himself after hearing it. Edward Grieg came especially to Paris and sat through the concert entranced. Afterwards Tom imitated the great Norwegian composer's strong accent when he spoke in English.

One of Tom's best platform tricks was his extraordinary ability to play the piano with his back to it, his hands behind him. Then he would play two different tunes with each hand and sing another, making a perfect blend of all three! He would imitate the mannerisms of de Pachmann, which some felt was part of the showmanship. He would talk to himself while on the platform, even stand up and applaud himself. Only those close to him knew that his moods in private would rival the kaleidoscope in their quick changes. Like de Pachmann he would pass rapidly from a state of great exhilaration to one of morbid depression.

Later on psychologists studied him because of the unprecedented way his great talents coincided with a low intelligence quotient—proving that perfection in piano playing could be attained without much conscious thought or any formal training. They concluded that Tom possessed a super-subconscious not given often to man and by which he was able to store limitless material in his memory. However, in spite of limited intellectual assets he composed a few pieces for the piano, one of them called the *Cyclone Galop,* a spirited dance in 2/4 time. But no human being before or since possessed his marvellous accuracy of ear and retentive musical memory.

On Tom's own accord most of his remuneration, which was considerable, was sent to help those of his race suffering from the ravages of the American Civil War. Tom never learned to read or write because he didn't need to. He was always surrounded by loving admirers who attended to all his requirements.

Public esteem for his uniqueness declined with the popularity of the phonograph, which had not been invented when Blind Tom's success began. Gradually his eccentricities increased with age and nervousness supervened. When he died on June 13, 1908 (aged 59) he was virtually forgotten.

Blind Tom died in Hoboken, New Jersey, where he had retired, cared for by a relative of General Bethune, who had since died. One might say that, like Beethoven, he died twice. He was pronounced dead by the doctor, which he seemingly was for about ten minutes. Then a sudden storm of tropic proportions began squalling outside. After

a bolt of frightening thunder Tom, like Beethoven on his
death-bed, awoke from his coma, sat upright, and shook
an angry fist at the direction of the sky. Then he fell back
dead, mourned by what few friends were left and by a
small fraction of the public that remembered the days of
his great fame.

The Watseka Wonder   III. 4

MY FIRST BOOK TO ATTRACT ATTENTION WAS
in the field of Psychic Phenomena. I read hundreds of
books and magazines on this subject to obtain my material,
and contrary to the claim of the Old World that the best
true ghost stories are on its side of the water, I am convinced that the most fascinating example I came across
happened in our Midwest. It occurred a short distance
from Chicago in the Spring of 1877, at Watseka, Illinois.

At the time it was given such publicity that the Psychi-
cal Research Society of London sent their own investigator,
Dr. Richard Hodgson. This specialist, a born skeptic,
came to the conclusion that the amazing case of Lurancy
Vennum was nothing less than one of spirit invasion.

The story begins on a cool evening the end of July, in
the home of Mr. and Mrs. Thomas J. Vennum, a modest
dwelling on the main street. They had lived there since
1875, having moved from Massachusetts with their twelve
year old daughter, Lurancy. Of a sudden they were dis-

turbed from their siesta by a hideous scream that came
from the child's room. Mrs. Vennum rushed in and found
her undergoing horrible convulsions. Her cheeks were
trembling and her face was distorted; the eyebrows and
forehead were contracted, as in a dark frown.

When Lurancy recovered consciousness, her entire personality had altered. The face, formerly characterized by
a dull woodenness of expression, had seemingly taken on
a relaxed sweetness, and the once listless eyes had
changed from furtive to straightforward glance. Even the
voice was not the same and had developed a warm rich-
ness of tone instead of its former monotonousness.

But most staggering of all things arising from her fit,
Lurancy now regarded everyone, including her parents, as
total strangers. She insisted that she was not their child,
referring to herself as Mary Roff and was unable to recall
any details of her life with them. Vaguely Mr. and Mrs.
Vennum had heard the name of Roff associated with an
elderly widow who lived some miles out of town, on a
farm. They had never met her and they gave this detail no
immediate significance until a doctor was called. After due
deliberation, he decided that Mrs. Roff be asked to come
and see Lurancy, hoping that by some accidental result
some light might be shed on the mystery of her condition.

In due course Mrs. Asa Roff came to call, and at once
Lurancy flung herself into the widow's arms with the
keenest emotion, asking the most knowing personal questions about her and calling her Ma. Naturally her real
parents were dumbfounded and felt deeply hurt at the
effusive affection with which she embraced Mrs. Roff, to
them a complete stranger. As their own child, Lurancy

had seemed incapable of sentiment of this kind and had remained undemonstrative.

Then it was that Mrs. Roff revealed that she had a daughter named Mary who had died about twelve years previously, the exact year that Lurancy was born. The child had been very delicate, and for the first years of her life Mrs. Roff and her late husband travelled in search of a better climate for her. A disease of the lungs, aggravated by cataleptic fits, eventually carried her off.

Significantly enough, ever since then Mrs. Roff had made efforts to communicate with Mary by Spiritualism and other ways of contact with the dead. Now she regarded the obsession of Lurancy Vennum as the realization of her dearest dream. She insisted that her daughter was reborn and that she could see a decided relationship in the two personalities, even in Lurancy's appearance itself. She had the same way of making gestures, the same graceful manner of doing things, also a walk that was half a run. In the words of Mrs. Roff, Lurancy possessed the similar hastiness of her Mary, who was always in a hurry —as if she knew her life on earth would be a short one.

Mr. and Mrs. Vennum were faced with the fact that their daughter's personality was now controlled by another, so on the physician's advice and Mrs. Roff's pleadings they agreed that the child be allowed to reside for the time being with her. Not only would it be a restful change for her but it would mean solace for the bereaved mother of Mary.

This was arranged, and not a day went by without her reborn child mentioning to Mrs. Roff little events that had occurred during her former existence on this planet. Re-

ferring to her early childhood when she had been taken to
Texas, she said one day: "Do you remember us crossing
the Red River and seeing all those Indians?" Or: "What's
happened to Mrs. Reeder's girls who lived next door to us
then?" On another occasion she picked out accurately a
place where she had buried her pet dog before she died
at Watseka.

Most curious of all was her absolute ignorance of time,
which she seemed totally unable to compute. A day, a
week, or a month were all the same to her. Sometimes she
did not appear to be aware of her own age. She came
across some of her old clothing in a trunk and identified
each piece. "There's the headdress I wore on my ninth
birthday. I must wear it again before it gets the moth." To
an old friend of Mrs. Roff she exclaimed: "You know,
Mrs. Lord, you have changed the least of anyone since
I went away."

Her sister, Minerva, two years older, who lived in Texas,
lost no time in coming to Watseka as soon as she heard the
strange news. When she arrived, the child caught her
around the neck, crying for joy: "Nervie, oh Nervie! Will
you play those hopping games we used to do?" Thus she
addressed her "sister" by the nickname when they were
children together.

Many other details came out which she could not possibly have heard from outsiders. Invariably she was upset
that people she knew before had grown old, whereas she
had remained the same. "Why don't you all manage to stay
young, like me?" she was fond of asking. Daguerrotypes
of Mary and Lurancy may be seen at Watseka which show
a strong physical resemblance of the two girls, and all who

had known Mary declared that the two personalities were very similar.

A brooding melancholy would come over the child in which she would hint that she had control of Lurancy's body only for a limited length of time. "I must kiss you often," she said one day to Mrs. Roff, "while I have lips to kiss with and arms to hug you."

On May 7, 1877 she fell into a deep depression and Mrs. Roff found her crying. Tears cascaded down her face as she told Mrs. Roff that the time had come for Lurancy to return to her own body again. Slowly she proceeded into a cataleptic seizure. A doctor was called, who claimed that the delirium was something quite alien to common catalepsy. The state of unconsciousness lasted about an hour, with the poor young girl assuming more and more the personality of Lurancy with each successive convulsion. In due course she became Lurancy. "Where am I? Where have I been?" were utterances she repeated and repeated.

Returned to her rightful parents, she never suffered another such incredible experience. In 1887 she married a farmer named George Binning, and she died in 1920. Mrs. Roff died shortly after she went into mourning a second time for a daughter whose return from the darkness of the tomb gave her a few weeks of utmost bliss.

The Mothers of America   III. 5

THE SOUL OF ANY COUNTRY IS CLOSELY TIED
to its women, who gave its children birth. Despite the
nasty innuendoes about Momism—played up by certain
American writers lately—it is not without significance that
on May 10, 1913 Congress set aside the second Sunday in
May for the observance of what is called Mother's Day.
The Resolution reads: "Whereas, the service rendered the
United States by the American mother is the greatest
source of the country's strength and inspiration, and

"Whereas, we honor ourselves and the mothers of
America when we do anything to give emphasis to the
home as the fountainhead of the State, and

"Whereas, the American mother is doing much for the
home, for moral uplift and religion, hence so much for
good government and humanity.

"Therefore, let it be RESOLVED that the President of
the United States is hereby authorized and requested to
issue a proclamation calling upon all government officials
to display the United States flag on all government buildings, and the people of the United States to display flags
at their homes and other suitable places on the second
Sunday in May, as a public expression of our love and
reverence for the mothers of this country."

Let us, therefore, ponder this charming and noble document which is unique to our country. Let the scoffers have their say—that America is too matriarchal. The fact remains that maternal love is the visible providence of our race. The pure and good thoughts a mother has implanted in the minds of her children continue to grow and manifest themselves long after she has gone. Even though everything else may die and become forgotten in her child, this memory is kept alive—as a token of which American children rise up and bless her on Mother's Day. It has been touchingly said that the loss of one's mother is one's first grief without her sympathy, and it is also the last real life-line of disinterested love. Fathers wish to be fathers of the mind of their children, as Emerson said—but the mother gives them their soul.

Great Americans have seldom failed to credit their maternal upbringing. Thomas Edison said: "My mother was the making of me. She was so true and sure of me. I felt I had something to live for—someone I must not disappoint." John Quincy Adams said: "I enjoyed perhaps the greatest blessing that can be bestowed on man—that of a mother who was anxious to form the character of her children rightly. Whatever my imperfections, they are mine not hers."

George Washington was eleven years old—the eldest of five children—when his father's death made his mother a widow. She administered his estate and brought up her children, educating them well with little money. From her, says one of his biographers, "he inherited his high temper and spirit of command."

Lincoln found that the death of his mother was the one grief in which she could not console him. In turn she once said that the one bright spot of her hard, unhappy life was the birth of her son, Abraham. To her natural instinct for upbringing, the world owes one of the most magnanimous men who ever lived. "All that I am, or ever hope to be, I owe to my angel mother," he once declared.

So let us burnish this charming document of Mother's Day each time the anniversary comes round. Let us urge American mothers to use the art of practical wisdom and wise judgment in upbringing their children. May mothers and children alike keep the pact of mutual dependency, befitting the spirit with which Mother's Day was made an Act of Congress.

It WAS, I BELIEVE, THE GREAT AMERICAN
writer O. Henry who wrote a story on the characteristic
phrase certain large American cities would utter could
they speak. New Orleans, he insisted, would say, "I used
to be." Philadelphia would murmur, "Perhaps." Chicago
would cry full-throated, "I will." But New York seems to
have flummoxed O. Henry. He confessed he did not know
its exclamation.

Not possessing O. Henry's rare imagination, I ought not
to venture where he left off. Yet I cannot resist speculating
on the voice of a few cities I know well abroad. Dublin
would intone, I feel, "Nothing matters." Paris would chirp
optimistically, "I give rebirth." Rome would beckon,
"Come unto me." London would whisper, "I preside." And
New York would fairly shout, "I overwhelm."

For just as London gazes down on one, New York
rushes up and leaves one speechless. Part of America she
certainly is (and she would be impossible anywhere else),
but she is not typical of the real America. New York's teeming population does not represent the masses but, oddly
enough, she is an important part of the American public.
More than in any other area of U.S.A. the New Yorker
is the nobody who's everybody.

Manhattan (an anagram of Indian phonetics meaning

"Celestial Country") grew upwards because it could not grow laterally. It changes so fast one is often left breathless after an absence. All the same, there is as much mystery to be found by the seeker as there is in the mountain fastnesses of Tibet. And this can be done by coming to terms with its past in juxtaposition with the present.

Let us begin with a survey from the top of a ranking skyscraper. As one goes heavenward by an elevator express, the influence of this device dawns upon one. It was invented in 1870 and only perfected at the turn of the century. You might call it the father of the modern skyscraper, for without it they could not be. With the popularization of the elevator, New York real estate went soaring. To think Peter Minuit bought all Manhattan once from the Indians for $24.00!

From atop you see at one glance how essential these tenuous towers of massive height are to the confined space of Manhattan. Bounded on the South, East, and West by the waters of the Bay (more like a Norwegian fjord) and both Hudson and East Rivers, the remarkable island is exceedingly small for a city compared to the size of London or Paris where the environs are endless. These 'scrapers are small cities in themselves, with their own police force, power plant, shops, and restaurants.

As you are swirled and eddied by the view into the miraculous ambiance of New York, observe this mute testimony to the God-given power in man to build. Every European enclave has its own shopping district. Like every city New York has several faces. When people talk of their New York, they usually mean their own corner of it. There is the New York of the New Yorker, for instance, who alone would satisfy his fellow-citizen in writing about it. There is the New York for those who come to savor it briefly. And unfortunately there is the New York of the slums, which gradually are being removed.

A quick tour of New York for the visitor would start at the Battery. Proceed up Broadway to Wall Street, which was named after a fence-line erected to keep cattle from straying. Stock Market wits suggest that more than fence would keep the Bulls and Bears at bay today! Somewhere in this street lived Captain Kidd, the Pirate, and wisecrackers insist that had he lived today he would perhaps have been a stockbroker. Another of doubtful reputation who resided here was Aaron Burr, a politician to whom we owe the formation of Tammany Hall. He lived here when Wall Street was considerably larger than it is today. Its dimensions are now one third of a mile long by forty feet wide.

The Street is remarkable for its statue of George Washington outside the Sub-Treasury Building, where he took the oath of office as President. The position for this statue is often criticized by foreign visitors because it is so near the scene where shekels are rattled, and they say he seemingly presides over the Stock Exchange opposite. Wall Street is of course presided over by Trinity Church, whose spire was once a great landmark in the City and which now is dwarfed by the towering buildings surrounding it.

Trinity Church nestles so snugly and charmingly within these canyons of buildings that its cemetery might escape notice altogether. Here, indeed, is a lucid piece of American history, and a few minutes will be rewarding, just to inspect the graves.

Here lies Richard Churcher, who died in 1691 in the

fifth year of his age. Nearby reposes William Bradford,
who printed the first newspaper in America. To remind
you that the Cemetery dates back to pre-Revolutionary
days over there is the headstone of John Watts, the last
Royal Recorder of Colonial America.

After absorbing the tranquillity here offered, continue
up Broadway to see historic City Hall, whose great dome
stands out boldly. When I first saw it as a boy, I felt that
I was being greeted by the apparition of an old and unex-
pected acquaintance, for it has a suggestion of a civic
edifice in London's City.

It is said that the Irish run New York and that the Jews
own it, so it is appropriate that the latter hold title to the
oldest Cemetery in the City at Chatham Square. A pilgrimage for Dutch visitors should be to St. Marks-in-the-
Bouwerie, where lies one-legged Governor Peter Stuyve-
sant. This district is a hive of activity every Sunday, as if
it were Saturday!

As you pass higher up the Island, it takes on the sense of
being a delightful combination of London, Paris and
Berlin. Greenwich Village, where inhabitants are so artistic
and vague that tomorrow means never, has the flavor of
Montmartre. Few New Yorkers realize the romance of
Seventh Avenue, which specializes in the manufacture
of the seductive whimsicalities of the eternal female—
where millions are made and lost yearly in fashion
speculation. It is one of New York's *recherché* features.

At Park Avenue and Forty-first Street General Washington had the narrowest escape of his life, when he was very
nearly captured by the British—and it is surely more than
coincidence that there are fewer accidents at this inter-
section (according to the Police) than any other in all

New York. Times Square, the nerve center of the City, is called the "Crossroads of the world," because you will surely run into everyone you know if you stand there long enough—or so they say. Here commences the Great White Way, "the greatest miracle in the world for those who cannot read!" as some wit has commented. As everywhere, stop-lights dazzle, and I sometimes think babies will soon be born with one eye green, the other red.

Times Square is not considered a fashionable part of New York in which to reside, but it is the most central. I am writing this book at a Hotel called Rosoff's within the heart of it. In what other city in the world can one step into five or six different worlds at once? Here you have close proximity to all theaters, restaurants, offices, railway stations, and department stores. Around the corner from my hotel is a bookstore open day and night. Not far away is that incredible institution called the New York Public Library. Times Square is a unique center for a city because it compresses so much within so small a space.

Watch for the pieces of daily poetry to be seen, such as the street pedlars, an entertainment in themselves. Very slick and dapper in the representation of their wares, the New York street vendor is unlike his counterparts abroad. He is usually young and well-dressed. You'll notice him walking along unobtrusively amid other pedestrians, carrying an umbrella although it isn't raining. Suddenly he brings himself up short, opens it and unfurls a large display of neckware and handkerchiefs, all competing in brilliant colors. And then his sales routine begins.

A running commentary issues from the man's glib tongue as he quickly gathers an audience. He sells many pieces because the price is low, but just as business is seemingly at its height he closes the umbrella as unceremoniously as he opened it, and quietly makes to leave. With his sixth sense he has spied a "cop" and his "shop" closes down, only to open again a few blocks away.

Time was when Fifth Avenue was full of stately residences of the so-called Four Hundred, when the social atmosphere was decorous. In what is left of New York "Society" (actually more like four thousand now!) people meet too often and there is never enough time allowed for them to accumulate value to each other. It has become like a hornet's nest, with its intrigues and petty feuds, nobody knowing who is speaking to whom. I must confess that I have had a better time at an Irish Wake than at many a New York dinner party.

Gone forever are the days when the social ladies would wear more clothes when swimming in the ocean than they did at the opera—when gentlemen kept on their white gloves while dining. Outside, the tallyho of the hansoms could be heard, and life in general flowed with persiflage and wit.

What scenes those famous lions outside the New York Public Library must have witnessed! They call to mind those which guard a certain building in Rome, said to roar whenever a virgin passes. What stories some of the old mansions could tell if walls had mouths. In the Fifth Avenue home of the once-famous hostess, Mrs. Cornelius Vanderbilt, there was a dinner party to end all dinner parties. "Her Grace," as the columnists called her, gave it to honor Count Bernstorff, the German Ambassador—and the time was a few days after commencement of World War One.

Mrs. Vanderbilt had issued her invitation to him well in

advance, in keeping with diplomatic custom; but when war was declared between France and England, she prayed that His Excellency would have the discretion to excuse himself. She soon learned that she was wrong, and that the crafty German had decided to brazen it out.

At dinner, conversation was strained and banal, and there was an interminable delay after the soup course. Bernstorff noticed that it had a slightly bitter taste, but he ate it to the dregs. Some time later he asked to be excused and all present were aware that the Count was seized with a vomiting attack.

To climax this embarrassment, the English butler appeared on the scene with a note unenveloped. It was signed by the Chêf, a patriotic Frenchman, and countersigned by the butler himself. It ran as follows: "The staff and myself have decided that we cannot serve any more dinner tonight. We refuse to serve a man who represents the enemy of our respective countries—so we are packing and clearing out immediately. Incidentally, we took the liberty of putting an emetic in His Excellency's soup!"

All this happened in a house now vanished, opposite St. Patrick's Cathedral, an edifice surrounded by dreaming spires and terraced palaces. It has its own aspect of eternity such as one feels on sight of European cathedrals. Somehow it has caught the spirit of the city, as if its spirit were the people's spirit. The companion on the Westside, the Protestant St. John-the-Divine, came into being Medieval-fashion—piece by piece. At first only sufficient money was available for the chancel (built in Byzantine mode). The funds were raised for a lovely Gothic nave, etc. & etc.

Rockefeller Plaza, where flowers and plants bloom overnight, is an unvaried delight the whole year round. Brownstone houses, with their high stoops (a remnant of Dutch architecture), appear in rows and rows in the side streets and make the words of Gropius (the German architect who designed Grand Central Station) ring true—that New York is united by her disunity of design.

Central Park contains a little-known Shakespeare garden, where blooms rosemary and rue and all the quaint plants mentioned in his plays—not forgetting mention of a most original and rollicking sculptural creation of the Mad Hatter's Tea Party. Walk diagonally across the Park to Grant's Tomb. Insure your life, then cross Riverside Drive to get the best view of the American Rhine. Ask yourself if any European city offers a better prospect. None do!

The Bronx (named after Jonas Bronken, a pioneer from Denmark who once owned most of it) boasts the old van Cortlandt Mansion (1748), also the Botanical Gardens with nearly thirty acres of bulging tropical flora under glass. These are intersected by the picturesque Bronx River, carved out during the Age of Glaciers, and they contain a Rock Garden which is a simulacrum of the *Jardin Alpin* in the Parisian Botanical Gardens. In the Bronx also is Rodman Drake Park, whose poet wrote long ago:

> "Yet I will look upon thy face again
> My own romantic Bronx, and it will be
> A face more pleasant than the face of man."

Irish-America   IV. 2

I HAVE ALWAYS BEEN PROUD THAT IRISH names have shone in every epoch of American history, especially in the struggle for freedom. To prove this one only has to visit Independence Hall in Philadelphia and look at the pictures. You will see at least ten Irish-Americans who signed the Declaration, notably Charles Carroll of Carrollton—a grey-haired dignified old gentleman with an aquiline nose and a broad sensitive brow.

Nearby is General Montgomery in blue uniform and lace ruffles, wearing his epaulettes. Not far away is Thomas Lynch of County Galway, whose boyish face and penetrating eyes, below his powdered wig, have been captured to perfection by a French artist. Here, too, are portraits of General Reed, Edward Rutledge, Matthew Thornton, Thomas McKean, James Smith and John Nixon—all owning Irish birth or ancestry. The man who announced the Declaration of Independence was Charles Thomson, born in Maghara, County Derry.

George Washington looked to Irishmen as a never-failing support. He was made an adoptive member of the Friendly Sons of St. Patrick in December, 1781. When accepting, he referred to the Society's "adherence to the glorious cause in which we are embarked." This group of brilliant Irishmen was made up of men of all religions, and had not most of them been born in Ireland, one of them might later have become President of the United States.

In it were such figures as General Knox of County Monaghan, the Secretary of War and Navy in the Washington Cabinet until 1794, also Captain John Barry of County Wexford, the first Commodore of the U.S. Navy— the founder of the American Navy. Another member was Colonel Richard Butler, a scion of the noted family of the Butlers of Ormonde, who fought with Washington in Saratoga.

Over and over again Washington acknowledged his debt to Irishmen who fought for Independence. "Ireland's cause is identical to ours," he once declared. He knew what is even now not generally known, that the early population of the American colonies was to a great extent Irish. On September 14, 1653 an order was made by the Commissioners of Ireland to the generals of Irish garrisons that they must supply "two hundred and fifty women of the Irish Nation above twelve years and not past forty-five; also three hundred men above twelve and under fifty years of age, to be found in Cork, Kinsale, Waterford, Youghal, and Wexford. All to be sent to transportation to New England." A little later English slave dealers transported about six thousand five hundred "Irish men, women, boys and maidens." Thus the Irish immigration to America began long before the potato famines of 1847-8-9.

The amazingly large number of American presidents with Irish blood have been much more directly descended in terms of generation than those of Anglo-Saxon ancestry. President Kennedy is third generation Irish-American, as

was President Wilson, who came of a Northern Irish Protestant family. Presidents Benjamin Harrison and Theodore
Roosevelt had Irish grandmothers and the parents of President Chester Arthur were born in County Antrim.

The grandfather of President McKinley was born in
Ballycastle, where he lies buried in lovely Bonamargy
Abbey. And the mother of President Cleveland was a Miss
O'Neal, the daughter of Abner O'Neal of Tralee. The
parents of Andrew Jackson came from Carrickfergus, and
other presidents who voiced their pride in being of Irish
descent were: James Monroe, Rutherford Hayes, James
Polk, Andrew Johnson, James Buchanan, and Ulysses S.
Grant.

"I'm proud of a little Irish blood on my mother's side,"
said President Lincoln in a recorded interview with my
ancestor, John O'Mahony, then in America to organize
support for the Fenian "Transatlantic Irishmen." The
President also spoke in praise and gratitude of the part
Irish soldiers were playing in Union successes. He was
well aware that upon the battlefields of Virginia, in the
cotton country of Georgia, and among the swamps of
Carolina, lay the bones of many an Irishman who had died
under the Stars and Stripes.

In the Civil War, as in the two World Wars, the Irish
upheld their reputation for military prowess. Lincoln
knew that the Irish population of America had declared
for the North preponderantly, also that over one hundred
and seventy thousand men of Irish birth or descent had
enrolled in the Union Army. The famed Irish Brigade,
commanded by the Irish-born General Thomas Meagher,
played a big part in the tragic battle of Fredericksburg.

In Ireland they claim that General Phil Sheridan was

born at Killinere, County Cavan, where a house still stands
which has a plaque on the wall: "Here was born Phil
Sheridan, 1830, Com-in-Chief U.S. Army." The Irish
answer to claims that he was born at Albany, New York
in 1831, is that he forged his American birth certificate!
They say that in order to be more certain that he would
obtain the promotion that would be the due of so brilliant
a soldier, he obtained an American certificate (easy to do
in those days) by swearing he was born in 1831—the year
his parents landed in America and when he was actually
one year old!

Be that as it may or may not, the Irish are happy to
admit that two of their greatest leaders were given to them
by America. President de Valera was born in New York in
October 1882 at a dwelling which once occupied the site
where the Chrysler Building stands today; and Charles
Stewart Parnell was the son of an American mother. Although born in Ireland, his grandfather was Commodore
Charles Stewart of the United States Navy and his forebears all American on his mother's side.

Haunting Memories   IV. 3

WHEN MY FIRST BOOK WAS PUBLISHED AND I
was preparing to go on the lecture platform, my friend,
Maurice Maeterlinck, who had written the Foreword,

said to me: "Now you are going to expand your personality, Patrick, and you will suffer. But you will gather a few happy memories along the way, if you are lucky . . ."

Looking back I realize that Maeterlinck's words came true. I did suffer unpleasantness, as for instance when I was appearing on a certain television interview. Bing Crosby had just undergone surgery and the lady who guessed correctly my vocation won his appendix in a bottle of alcohol as the prize!

Nor did I relish very much the time when Maeterlinck and I were leaving his New York hotel one day for luncheon. A fashionably dressed lady came up to him and took his hand. This was not surprising and he was used to kindly demonstrations from his fans, who remembered his *Blue Bird* play, which was once so famous American manufacturers even named products after it.

"Oh, Mr. Maeterlinck," she said politely. "I've just been told who you are, and I must tell you how much I am still enjoying my *Blue Bird* refrigerator."

Fortunately the great Belgian writer could not understand English, although he read it deeply. How could I translate such an unintentional broadside? And so I told him that the lady wished to compliment him on his work, and that she had also asked me the way to Madison Avenue. Eyeing me suspiciously he asked: "Why did she go off in the wrong direction?"

In my travels as an American writer, the two most unforgettable characters I have met were not American. But because they had pertinent things to say about my country, and also because I would not have met them without being an American citizen, I include them here. One, you will have guessed, was Maeterlinck. The other was Bernard Shaw. These friendships alone have made me a memory millionaire!

Today the name of Maurice Maeterlinck is not so famous, but his time will surely come again. It has been well said that he did for the spirit what Shaw did for the intellect. With thoughts as wide as the sky and as deep as the sea, he brought a new thrill to the theater and liberated it from the moribund reality of Ibsen and Strindberg. The fact that he wrote the libretto for the great lyrical drama *Péllèas and Mélisande* makes him one of the master-singers of the world. He was the first writer to see the poetry in the bee, the pantomime, and mysticism.

He was a shy genius who shunned publicity, lived a cloistered existence in France. When he came to America for the first performance of the *Blue Bird* opera at the Metropolitan in 1923, blue birds fluttered in the streets to welcome him, and ladies wore emblems of them on their hats. But when he came again in 1940, a refugee from the Nazis who held his name high up on the Gestapo List for his anti-German writings in World War One, the reception was one of apathy.

The poet and his wife arrived from Portugal, where they had gone to avoid the Germans who were then going through France like an express train. They arrived in New York with much baggage, plus two blue parakeets—pets of Madame Maeterlinck. The birds were seized by the American Customs in accordance with the animal health laws, and the incident received quite a play in the press. Of course Madame Maeterlinck was inconsolable.

Not long afterwards, they received a letter from a nine year old girl in Milwaukee. She had read of the poet losing his birds and wrote asking if she might come to New York with her mother and bring her own blue birds, as she could not bear the thought of him being without his own. So the child came and a little ceremony took place at which she gave to the famous writer the blue birds in a cage constructed to the specifications of that which was used for the bird owned by Tyltil and Mytil in the *Blue Bird* play.

This incident remained one of Maeterlinck's cherished memories during his stay in the United States. It was the sort of kindliness that would only be likely to occur in America and made Maeterlinck feel at home. Home for a poet is not necessarily where he was born. It is where his ideas are. Maeterlinck was born in Ghent, but he preferred to live in France. He learned to appreciate America, but men of his age do not export to new lands with ease. I was his literary assistant for five wonderful years.

When I knew him, he was a somewhat faded lion. He had indeed seen everything and the reverse of everything. Once he commented in reply to my remark that it must be gratifying to be fully recognized in one's own lifetime: "Yes, it is. And I have lived so long that I have seen some of my friends, who had stones thrown at them when alive, get even larger stones raised to eulogize their memories after death!"

His mind was the most universal, the most encompassing, I have ever known. Nor do I expect to meet anyone again with such insight and outlook. I can see him now, in my mind's eye, as we parted for the last time. He looked very *racé*, a tall and handsome old Fleming, with a brow sensitively curved, always a little hidden beneath a rebellious forelock which gave the finishing touch to the look of the poet. He and his wife were leaving by ship to return to Nice. Reporters crowded outside his cabin before sailing time, but Maeterlinck didn't want to be interviewed: "Just tell them that I am an old man going home to die," he said to me.

I urged that he write a few lines for me to hand the gentlemen of the Press, and taking pencil in hand he wrote on a blank telegraph form: "I leave, but do not quit, America; America that will remain ever in my heart; America the Custodian of Peace, the Trustee of Civilization."

That same year, in the summer of 1946, I went to interview Bernard Shaw for an American publication. As I made my way to his home at Ayot St. Lawrence in Hertfordshire (now known as Shaw's Corner), I felt a sense of trepidation. I had read interviews he had given to more or less prominent writers, some of whom made him appear very overbearing. I had the impression that he had directed his own life ruthlessly, like one of his own plays—without too much regard for the supporting players. Therefore I didn't expect any special consideration. But to me he was courteous and kind.

In person he looked more elegant and healthier than his photographs conveyed. He possessed in a marked degree that air which is the stigmata of genius. Smiling benignly from the tufts of white whiskers on each side of his ruddy face—to which horn-rimmed spectacles gave an owl-like effect—he began in the friendliest manner. "So you want to take a tour of Bernard Shaw. Have you ever taken a tour of yourself?"

Cocking his beard in an engaging manner, he then proceeded to interview me. What was my attitude to religion?

How were my relations with women? In what way would I have been spending my life if I hadn't become a writer? To all this I stammered replies as best I could.

All the time I was studying Shaw deeply—this man who always got the better of any argument and managed to make everyone accept his views with no less nonchalance than if he were feeding them ice cream. Only the heart and eyes were young, but in a miraculous moment I saw the years fall away from his wrinkled face and before me sat the young Shaw I had read about—the lad who refused aid from his teachers and buried himself in books, insatiably absorbing knowledge day and night.

My first question was concerning his views on the modern generation. Fixing his basilisk eyes upon me, he railed against it melodiously in that charming brogue which clothed his speech. "In my younger day the right people fetched up with the right people and lived comparatively happily together. Today, unsuitable people run after other unsuitable people like mice upon a treadwheel. They marry and divorce, and so the mouse-race goes on!"

Hands upon his knees, clasping them a little shakily, he continued: "I am called an angry old man, but it is not enough to be angry in a good cause. There is always something strongly suspicious in a keen antipathy of good to bad—and that is why my satirical scalpel searches continually for the trace of an approaching Millennium."

I expressed admiration for his dramaturgy. "Few people realize that my plays begin where they end and end where they begin," he said with an humorous glimmer in his eyes. "Each one supplements the other and is only a part of a mightier structure. I believe that art should be ar-

tistic, but theater need only be theatrical up to a point.
I try to make people think, and if I do not succeed, at
least I have made them think that they have thought after
seeing any of my plays."

As he finished speaking, an elderly lady entered the
room. It was Mrs. Shaw and she greeted me warmly.
Shaw reacted immediately. "You sit down and talk to
Charlotte," he ordered. "And because you are Irish, Patrick, I am going to write this interview for you. It'll be
safer that way . . ."

Suiting his actions to his words, he went to his desk
while I opened conversation with Mrs. Shaw on Shaw.
"He's got a mind that emanates like radium," she said.
"How can it be analyzed?" I asked what was the greatest
factor in his creative faculties. "Irish discontent," she
snapped with finality. "Shaw is never satisfied with what
he produces and always seeks to better it."

In what seemed a trice, Shaw was back, walking the
full length of the room waving a couple of sheets of paper.
"Here is what I want you to tell my American friends
about me. After I am dead you'll be able to sell this little
manuscript for ten pounds." (There he was wrong; I only
got five!)

Taking me by the arm, he led me through the door
which gave into the garden, very English and modest—
contrasting in charm with the ugliness of the house's exterior. "I want you to see the Shaw who loves his little
piece of England. I never felt at home in Ireland, you
know. All that mendicity and mendacity depressed me."

I suggested that being Irish had influenced him enor-
mously. "Yes, of course. My Irish nature has always driven
me from one extreme to another which has made every

play I have written a reflection of a shifting intellectual experience." Somehow we then touched upon reciprocal relations, from which I had much suffered lately. I found Shaw so sympathetic that I unburdened some of it.

"Contrary to most Irishmen," he confided, "my Irish temperament has much more to do with inspiration than with pure rage in matters of this kind. I have put up with the derelictions of friends for so long I have invented a formula of cure which works wonders. When anyone behaves in an ungentlemanly way to me, I come out here —in the open air. Then I look up at the sky and I say to myself: 'Shaw, thank heaven there's a Gentleman up there.' "

Pretending to be an atheist was, therefore, merely part of his diverse and contrary nature! My last contact with him was by way of one of his famous postcards. I had sent him a golden shamrock on his ninetieth birthday, and at the same time I asked him for his views on England, then in the hands of a Labor Government. He fired back with: "England can afford to go broke. America cannot. She must be prepared to keep the entire Western World. Thanks for the Shamrock. I will wear it until I myself drop off of it!"

Which of course he did on November 2nd, 1950.

Replying to Our Critics   IV. 4

OUR DETRACTORS INVARIABLY CALL AMERICA
materialistic in a derogatory sense. Of course they resent
the fact that we are more successfully materialistic than
they are! We are indeed materialistic in the sense that
we like our ideas put in material form. We must have
things presented in such a way that they appeal to all
five senses at once. What's wrong with that?

That brilliant and perceptive Judge Sewall (the American Pepys) underscored this point when he wrote in his
diary, describing a visit to the lady of his heart: "I got
my chair in place, had some converse—but very cold and
indifferent it was. Asked her to acquit me of rudeness if
I drew off her glove. Enquiring the reason, told her it was
great odds between handling a dead goat and a living lady.
Off came the glove!"

There is a great and general wish with Americans to
get to the basis of things and look facts squarely in the
face. They once looked Monarchy in the face and it vanished to make way for the free man. Since then, what
matters most about an American is not what he has or who
his family is—but what he can do by way of ability.

The next line of attack is usually against the conformity
of the American, who is really at heart an individualist.
This is proved by the vehemence with which he dislikes

constraint or being told what to do. Contrary to the trend in some foreign lands, nationalization of industry (or any move that smacks of confiscation) is regarded here with alarm. The average American will tolerate much but reacts quickly against the tamperings with the rights of others—especially those associated with property.

In a subtle way the American is thus only living up to the idea of equality enunciated in the Declaration of Independence. Liberty, equality and fraternity hold their own very well in this area. Even the man who has little himself is ready to guard the havings of others with all the jealousy he might give to them if they were his. Unlike in Europe, we grow up without any feeling of inferiority, and this is the secret why wealth in others does not arouse envy. Moreover, everyone knows it is accessible to all who wish to make the effort to earn it. The menial laborer is as sure of himself and his chances to achieve what he wants as the University student is certain he will reach his particular goal. Both know that those at the top are keenly on the lookout for hard workers.

Thus we have an easy familiarity between rich and poor found nowhere else in the world and one of the hardest aspects of the American way for foreigners to understand. They cannot fail to notice that this spirit disarms jealousy and encourages hope in a manner that would be impossible in a class-ridden society. It should be clear that for the average American the wealth of others is merely a symbol of everyone's future chances, that he will not aid and abet the diminution of its sanctity in any way.

Some foreign critics dwell on what they call the ruthlessness of Big Business. Only those familiar with inter-

national affairs would understand that this ruthlessness is
a duty to the public for the cheapening of production.
Sentiment cannot be permitted to stand in the way of
turning out the best product at the lowest cost—and the
great test in business everywhere is to make profits and
to please all concerned. It cannot be entirely without
coincidence that the creation of the spinning machine, the
steam engine, and the power loom occurred at about the
same time as the Declaration of Independence.

For someone who does not know the difference between
a bill of exchange and a debenture, it seems to me that
any sane American must believe in more and more Big
Business so that America will go round better and better.
But there are those in office who would almost like to re-
peal the laws of supply and demand! They think in terms
of bureaucracy and verify Parkinson's law—that bureaucracy breeds more bureaucracy. They cannot see that business is the most democratic of all pursuits and must remain
the American democratic image.

I have seldom met an enterprising American who has
a good job and who doesn't intend to change it eventually
—especially if promotion doesn't come with the rapidity
he feels is in order. One senses that continually there is
going on in the minds of energetic young Americans a
veritable search for the wisest course to promote a career.
In foreign countries a young man enters a firm as a clerk,
and there he will likely remain until the end—with a small
amount of promotion along the way, if he is lucky.
Whereas in America, he may take the same type of job
and appear later in a newspaper office, then perhaps as
an assistant to an Undertaker—or even as a process server
for lawyers! Somehow he may graduate from this and in

the prime of life may rise to being a Member of Congress —and finally be elected to the board of a large Corporation.

No possibility stands in the way of a man's legitimate aspiration. Failure in America is never complete, never irredeemable. More often than not, failure in one type of business may be the stepping stone to another in which success is achieved.

In business the American will likely have interests in every quarter of the land, thus he knows every part of it —the economic conditions, habits and character, and even the varying anthropologies in all parts. To recall the words of Calvin Coolidge that the business of America is business, reminds us that business here is a great gatherer and holds the country together in a special sense.

Carping critics think that Americans live too much in the future, pursuing life too avidly so that we give ourselves insufficient time to enjoy the present through rumination of the past. They have no concept of our free enterprise competition, in which nothing recedes faster than one's last success. Unlike in Europe, where a famous man in any field remains famous, the American counterpart must be continually renewing himself. A writer must be trying to win new audiences, an actor constantly changing his personality as much as possible. In no vocation can one feel safe in just coasting along on a glamorous past. In the implacable competition of the American way, the race is to the swift.

All visitors to our shores agree that America is the country of the future. Those who come under its spell feel that they have landed onto another planet. There is a far more noticeable change from the variation one feels when

travelling from Europe to the Orient. Many a visitor to
these shores has found himself temporarily imbued with
that restless American nervous energy, that quickness of
mind to find expedience.

What a difference when one goes to France! Although
you travel only a few thousand miles, you have truly
traversed millions of miles spiritually. You come to the
conclusion that the French are as alien to us as the Chinese
are to the Californians. They do not give a curse for any
other nationality in the world, and they make no secret
of this. They may be attracted to you in an impersonal
way, but to the average American they are not attracted.

Cerebrally they respect our pocket-books, but our personality does not appeal. In fact there are some leaders
in the rarefied atmosphere of Parisian society who boast
they have never had an American darken their hearths!

What an amazing people! They erect statues in order
to have the pleasure of destroying them in due course.
They are always crying "Long live somebody" or "Down
with so-and-so." Their language is very voluptuous, and
contains so many cut-and-dried sentences that every
French fool can give the impression of being clever!

My own satiric image of Madame France is portrayed
by a stout, formidable woman seated at a high cash desk,
using calculated cunning to add another few francs onto
my bill—perhaps even adding in the date when she thinks
she can get away with it! If, as some wit has suggested,
the English are honest individually but pickpockets col-
lectively, the French are honest as a race but pickpockets
individually! One day I hope they will master the art of
separating a tourist from his money with a certain amount

of legerdermain. It is not their greed for money that one minds, but the continual lusting after gratuities.

I believe I can safely say that America is the least tippable country I know. Those clamorously keen on tips are usually recent immigrants, not yet Americanized. People who render tippable service in America are generally paid enough that they don't care if they receive a tip or not —whereas in France no one seems to be paid enough!

There is a clever rumor, manufactured perhaps by the Madison Avenue boys, that French women are more stylish than others. Many an American woman goes to Paris with an inferiority complex. She fears that the French are more knowledgeable about Art and Literature, that they are better talkers.

Somehow the Frenchwoman does manage to seem more vivacious than others elsewhere, but to me she is like those special wines which we all like to taste but which are not acceptable as table beverage. One must marvel at the way they handle their birthdays. The years they take off their ages are never lost. The Frenchwoman adds them to the ages of women she does not like!

The average American soon gives the lie to the witticism that good ones go to Paris when they die. He returns to his home town or city realizing that it is really the better of the two, ready to kiss the American earth. This is forcibly brought out in the story of the tourist who took a tour of the Père Lachaise Cemetery in the French Capital. After seeing the many shrines erected to the departed great, he was asked what he thought of it. "Not much," he replied. "I prefer graveyards where I know the folks."

This man was right in his way. The simple things are

always easier to understand and it is these that are more precious for our memory storehouse. Having lived abroad these past few years, my appreciation for substantive American things has increased and I can agree with this man's sigh.

The English critic is usually the most vocal behind our backs. He finds it hard to adapt to the surrealism of American life and does not make a good citizen (as a matter of fact, few take out First Papers according to statistics). They find fault with the kindly inquisitiveness of Americans and resent being asked good-natured questions by people they hardly know. They feel this to be a probing into their personal lives.

In their insular upbringing such questions are considered in poor taste. And if you took them to task for thus missing out on much good conversation which must commence with personal queries, they would likely retort that in being insular they are merely exercising their natural right—very much the same way the American uses his Declaration of Independence to explain to himself his particular approach to gregariousness. They might likely infer that just because no one else behaves in their particular way is sufficient reason for an Englishman to do so!

There is a story, obviously apocryphal, which drives this home. An American soldier in England during the last War entered a compartment aboard one of those antique English trains in search of a seat. The compartment was full except for one space. But on closer inspection he saw that it was occupied by a small dog owned by an elderly spinster. The lady was holding onto it with a protective hand and when the soldier asked her to take the animal onto her lap so that he might use the space, she became most indignant. She insisted that the dog was entitled to the seat as much as any human being.

The soldier tried some gentle suasion but without success. Losing grip on himself, he peremptorily took up the animal and hurled it out of the train window. The spinster went into hysterics, as well she might; and after she had calmed down, a purple-faced Englishman, whose nose had been buried in a newspaper, looked up and commented: "You Americans are a funny lot. You drive on the wrong side of the street. You eat with your fork in the wrong hand. And now you've just thrown the wrong bitch out of the right window!"

If the story were true, I'm sure the American soldier would merely have lifted the dog from the seat, and placed it on the lady's lap. But it does show up some amusing anachronisms. Over there they drive on the left, although most of the remaining world uses the right. They disregard logic by ignoring the decimal system used in almost all other countries. They divide their pennies into four farthings (which are now so valueless they have been abandoned), and their shillings into twelve pence. They still measure distance in rods and furlongs, both of which contain an unequal number of feet. And the Englishman is served a drink of whisky which has to comply with a seventy-second part of a kilderkin. Perhaps that is why there'll always be an England?

Our brethren across the water invariably attack what they call American uniformity, and at least one nasty English author nicknamed America the "Babbit Warren." It does not occur to them that they mistake uniformity for a weakness instead of the virtue that it is. How else would fifty "Sovereign States within a Sovereign State" hang together as well as they do? It is merely another form of solidarity.

When I went to school in England, they told me that American history was too short to warrant a place on the curriculum. But in my own study of it I have found it to be a great romance of humanity, written on the clean pages of a New World. Only the myopic person could read it and not admire the great multitudes of talented men and women who acted it out.

We are criticized abroad for not using English-English, which has lost much of its graphic power through the invention of many American idioms. Even the anti-American Oscar Wilde was forced to admit that our "slanguage" has borrowed from the best of literature in some instances. He recalled that when he was on his lecture tour in the West, a man referred to another as having "painted the town red," which Wilde recognized was borrowed from Dante's *Divine Comedy*. He might also have remarked that the common expression "You said it" comes directly from the Bible. Jesus often used "Thou saith it." If we think about it, we are all artists who have the opportunity to paint our word canvas well or badly.

Fortunately, in the last analysis, common differences are more binding than common similarities, and it is only human to judge others by one's own standards. In spite of these exacting critics, they are forced to admit that America is not a frivolous nation, that she possesses enduring qualities in order to come to world leadership.

Secretly, if not overtly, they have to award us general esteem for no other reason than that the spirit of our originality startles them. A comprehensive tour of our vast

Continent would be for these gentlemen what braille must
be for the blind!

Things to Hope for   IV. 5

LATELY I WAS TALKING TO A FRIEND WHOM I
regard as a patriotic American-born citizen. In the course
of our conversation, he remarked: "The trouble with
America today is that she has no purpose in the world. We
are, moreover, losing faith in our own omnipotence. Some
of us are losing pride because we are no longer given the
respectful affection we feel we deserve from the rest of
the Western world . . ."

I countered that even the great Alexandre de Tocque-
ville exaggerated our shortcomings when he paid his
memorable visit these many years ago. He forecast catas-
trophies which never occurred and are now not likely to
happen. I could have quoted a letter George Washington
wrote to John Jay in 1787, at which time he said: "Among
men of reflection few will be found, I believe, who are not
beginning to think that our system is more perfect in
theory than in practise; and that notwithstanding the
boasted virtue of America, it is more than probable we
shall exhibit the last melancholy proof that our people
are not so competent to their own government without the
means of coersion in the Sovereign."

That must have been one of his "off" days, but it only goes to show that it is necessary to take long views of America's future and not to focus on the smaller problems in the foreground. It is always darkest before dawning, and the Father of his Country soon found this out.

Returning to my depressed friend, I suspect that he was quoting some fanatical news columnist who doesn't have his finger on the pulse of America. For those who want to think originally, an indifference to the newspaper editorials should be acquired. Indeed, talk of this kind could end in contributing to a most unfavorable estimate of us in the minds of foreigners. Personally I strenuously deny that America has lost her purpose in the world or that we need feel any less pride in the world's appreciation of us as a nation.

That does not mean we should ever avoid indulgence in self-analysis. Our way of life should expose itself continually to inner criticism, always aimed at self-improvement. However, the best kind of criticism demands that a man not resist his reason but that he uses it. For some inexplicable reason gloom will always be the newspaper's most popular commodity to peddle rather than cheer. Good news always seems to be consigned to back pages!

If I have any fear about America, it is that we may fall a victim to the crankiness of certain over-zealous patriots who confuse their own personal prejudices with love of country. Until one fully understands the mental and spiritual processes that begat America, the devotion one has within is not easy to give. True patriotism goes beyond lip-service, and I venture to say that some of the greatest American heroes have died unsung—their real reward being higher than this poor world can give.

The history of the world's errors is made up mainly of a long and dreary list of missed opportunities—a knack of not noticing the writing on the wall. All countries are to blame in this, but the great strength of America has always been in its ability to take (and perhaps neglect) criticism from foreign sources, also to be the sternest critics of ourselves. In speaking of what we may hope for, I am reflecting comments by other writers I have read, or pieces of public speeches by politicians—even stray remarks overheard in after-dinner conversations.

One does not have to be clairvoyant to realize that we are now facing a situation which can only be dubbed as mass boredom. One cannot fail to feel a little shattered by the sullen faces one sees each day in the streets of any large American city. They look as if they are without interest in anything save such diversions as television and an illusive dance after pleasure. Nothing remarkable is left for them except the flatness of the world, and curiosity has destroyed whatever was curious and alluring.

Mass boredom is just as terrifying a threat as Nuclear War and can easily turn man into evolution's worst failure, loathing his push-button work—whatever it happens to be. It will confront every successful materialistic nation sooner or later. The lesson to be learned is a very old one: that when people achieve the desires of their hearts, the dynamic of their lives evaporates. It proves, too, that we cannot get out of technocracy any more spirituality than we put into it.

I have no quarrel with automation in itself. No one would deny that it has brought the world great benefits; it has lightened human toil and has saved manufacturing costings to an enormous degree. On the debit side, there

is the danger of a mechanized type of man emerging—
and this danger must be watched. Man must remain master
of himself if he is to remain free in the strictest sense of the
word—for the supremacy of mind and the equality of man
are really indivisible.

The present trend of automation, based upon the stern
discipline demanded by the machine from human beings,
is alarming. In some cases you hear of it ordering men
about with callous rigidity. Just a casual visit to any large
factory leaves the impression that as machinery appreci-
ates man depreciates. Serious thinkers on this subject, such
as the psychologist, Erich Fromm, fear that *Robotism* may
engulf man in a catastrophe of insanity and chaos. The
only solution to this danger is to rely on automation in
such a way that we can do without it at any time this
danger lurks.

There is a good story, grafted onto a leader of a new
African State (he could not have been Dr. Nkrumah because he had a sense of humor!). He was being shown a
motor car factory in Detroit and, after witnessing one
piece of automated operation after another he was taken,
somewhat dazed, into an elevator to the restaurant for
some refreshment. In the course of the upward journey
one of the passengers, a flippant employee, pinched the
female elevator operator in the posterior. The African
leader heaved a sigh of relief. "Thank the Lord," he said
gleefully, "that something around here is done by hand!"

Ridiculous as the story may sound, it does drive home
a point. The fame and success of our automated machinery
will never move the world in our favor. As the African
felt about it, the routine of its mechanism numbs the

minds of countless people, who thus lose a sense of flexibility and adaptability.

What is the way out? Fortunately, specialists insist that only one part of the brain is affected. That part of the mind, which forms the majesty of man, is not. It waits there to be developed like an unused muscle for the attainment of inner tranquility for anyone with the willingness to cultivate.

Throughout the ages, all the sages from Aristotle onwards have stressed that the company of one's self should be an omnipresent delight—that the hours passed alone should stand out like mountain peaks. For there is a little loneliness needed for the soul of man to flower. In order to combat the dangers of mass boredom brought on by robotism and hedonism, there is one sure way which psychiatrists never suggest because it would do them out of work. I refer to cultivating the urge for an inner life. Indeed, the very hope of man now resides in his capacity to come to terms with this form of abstraction, which need not interfere with his devotion to family or society.

Many are already discovering, by taking stock of eternal values, that their happiness is really the outside world transfigured by spiritual vision. In this sense each man *is* an island. We are all forced sooner or later to live in a microcosm of our own creating. It can be good or bad, hideous or beautiful—according to our creation of it. Mental adventure is the only approach to this inner contentment, and it must be self-created.

Aristotle, in his philosophy, saw man's development in three stages: Prehistoric man, wholly guided by instinct; then historic man, led by his intellect—of which he con-

sidered himself a product. And far into the corridor of
time he envisioned the Man of the Future, whose fulfill-
ment would be found in the Kingdom of the Soul. This
man will inherit the earth and so will the nation he belongs to.

Anticipating such a man was John Donough, whose
grave I came across in the shadow of New Orleans Cathedral. His *hic jacet* is dated 1899, and he was a successful
American merchant, whose rules of life he ordered cut on
his head-stone:

"Remember that labor is a condition of existence."
"No one is perfect, therefore do not expect too much."
"Praise when you can, blame only when you must."
"Prepare to be crossed and disappointed every day."
"Do your share of labor when it comes your way."
"Attribute good motives to others when you can."

Surely here was a man well aware that the American
spirit must stand firmly on its own base, resting its claim
on the bedrock of human nature.

There is a creeping danger enlightened psychologists
are warning against. They say that sentimental pleasures
are too much being superseded by those that are mechanical. It may sound trite to say that many these days
become housebound with radio and television programs,
but when they do get to the countryside it is even worse.
Invariably they go by motor car from which they do not
leave except to go to a rest room, and even then do little
or no walking.

Psychologists say that these mechanistic pleasures,
which are all right in proper moderation, create mainly a

feeling of want rather than the inner refreshment we need. In a curious way—by doing away with effort—these mechanistic pleasures actually increase boredom.

Every psychologist is, of course, familiar with the type of boredom which overtakes the pleasure-loving classes who are often too rich to wish to learn the life of the mind, and in whom the capacity of enjoyment lessens with the years. All too frequently these people become dependent upon full-fledged psychiatrists against whom they are sometimes left defenseless.

No one can prevent the process of ageing (and old age can turn into what can be compared with a work of art). Just because our bodies have to grow old, is it necessary for the mind to keep pace? Everyone has within the ability to keep the mind young, although physical equality would seem to end in all careers at sixty-five. Such a rule is certainly open to censure, but since it is firmly entrenched, let us ponder the words of ex-President Hoover on the subject of retirement. This worthy American once said:

"There is no joy to be found in retirement except from some kind of productive work. Otherwise you degenerate into grumbling to everybody about your pains and ills and Income Tax. The other oldsters will want to talk about theirs, yet anyone who keeps at part-time work has something worth talking about. He has a zest for the morning paper and three meals a day. The solution is to be found in obtaining a job where your skills and experience get exercise. And America needs skill and experience."

I often hear it proposed to do such-and-such a thing to kill time. Killing time is a form of suicide. Between time and us, it is as to which shall kill the other! But Mr. Hoover knows of what he speaks because his regime ushered in a new era—or was itself present at its birth —in which the individual has since been threatened by the group. Individuals can never successfully be treated as groups of people, and American idealism must always be concerned with the fate of the individual.

Just to be promised more and more prosperity is hardly enough to keep the average man alive spiritually, retired or not. To do this he must become increasingly aware of himself as an individual. It is altogether possible that the conquest of Space will help to accomplish this. Our spiritual dimensions are bound to increase now that we know the Universe belongs to everyone for the free play of energy, spiritual and physical.

Paradoxically, in spite of this mechanized age, mechanical expressions such as *Please* and *Thank you* are considered these days so automated that they no longer carry the essential kindliness. This answer has been given to me lately when I have noted their omission in heavily urbanized districts—usually by those who seek a general sanction for their own poor manners. No one would claim that these mechanical observances of courtesy make the man, but they do make him more agreeable. Personally, I love to hear the essentially American expression "You're Welcome," which is a poem in itself.

Foreign visitors are quick to note here the lack of traditional formalities, which are fostered abroad. While they agree that American hospitality is more heart-warming than anywhere else in the world (and Southern manners the most sensitive), they miss the old-world formalities. They are pleasantly alarmed by the back-slapping familiarity and frankness of people they may meet in the West and mid-West, but what charms them most is the American genius for making them feel immediately at home.

Perhaps a revival of old-fashioned formality would help us to be better understood by Europeans who come to America. Over there they make any meeting the subject of extensive preliminary greetings. Before discussing a business deal they will touch upon the weather, or mutual acquaintances—or some other facet of mutuality that might be far removed from the reason for the meeting. Only after these commonplaces is an important matter broached.

This may sound useless and superficial to some of us, whose pace is more rapid, but it does serve a purpose. Such digressions often pave the way for better mutual understanding and may even preclude a possible disagreement later on. When Europeans negotiate with us they sometimes find us a little too straightforward. They observe that we have little hesitation in letting them know what we think, using a bluntness which can nonplus. This criticism is so easy to remedy. Worldly wisdom consists, in the last analysis, of respecting futilities—little pieces of finesse which assist reciprocal relations.

Of course, in being frank and blunt, the average American might retort that he is merely living up to his concept of the Declaration of Independence—that principle which enshrines the equality of man. Let cynics have their say —that it is useful mainly for Fourth of July orators— Americans *are* created equal within the meaning of this noble idea. We all have equal opportunities and privileges, and every native born American is heir-apparent to the throne in the White House (in spite of current rumors

that one must be the son of a millionaire to occupy it,
I'm sure the day will dawn again when the choice will be
made from the humble and highly-gifted).

Such knowledge of equality helps Americans to think
independently, to develop a personality within the limitless limitations of this premise. It has, I believe, founded
the free enterprise system and has helped to make Capital-
ism such a success. Corporations such as American Tel.
and Tel. could never exist without it because there are not
enough millionaires to support them, and all corporations
rely on the investment from the savings of the little man.
This may sound trite, but not everyone is aware of it.

Unfortunately there are those—and today they are becoming more numerous—who feel that the fact they were
born equal entitles them to a free living. They envy the
success of others and do not seemingly appreciate that it
depends upon an ambition to make a pact with equality.
It cannot guarantee equal results, and the degree of success depends upon us.

Just the idea of equality has attracted thousands of
talented people to these shores and it is a wonderful experience to meet a new immigrant who has fallen in love
with the ideology of America. I had that delight recently
when I met quite accidentally a refugee from an Iron
Curtain country. He had that beam in the eye of someone
who had come under a spell, as if some flutter had passed
across his heart like a great white bird. I found myself
revelling with him as he was breathing in the atmosphere
of freedom, such as he had never known before. He was
now in a land where there was no restraint such as he had
known behind the lines of suppression. For the first time

he was able to talk to anyone he wished and needed to feel no fear. He was in the land of the free and the home of the brave! What delight to witness a man freed from political bondage and thoroughly vocal of appreciation for a new way of life.

This man told me that he had begun his way up the ladder of success by taking a post as a domestic servant, fully convinced that he would not have to remain in it very long. It was a temporary post he had no difficulty in obtaining. Fairly well educated and clearly a man of ability, he saw nothing degrading in doing service for others.

Why is it, I asked myself, that most Americans see something *infra dig* in domestic service? After all, nine out of ten of us take orders from someone else in one way or another. I would say that nine out of ten of us find that our work requires doing certain things which we do not relish, but which those in authority find necessary to request.

The American servant, if one can be acquired, is unique to this world. It was indeed a stroke of American genius that thought of substituting the word Help for Servant. There is also a touch of genius in the way a domestic servant is never made to feel any sense of inequality. There is an easy familiarity between employer and employee, as human being to human being. Reciprocal relations have been dignified in this area to a high degree and I cannot ever see why domestic work is considered menial and therefore obnoxious to Americans. To emphasize the servant crisis here are a couple of good stories, totally without foundation. That famous playboy, the late Prince

Aly Kahn once asked the superintendent of the Gentlemen's washroom of a Hollywood hotel if he knew of a
valet who might be seeking a post.

"Sorry, Sir," the man replied. "Actually I'm looking for
one for myself, and cannot find any."

Then there is the one about President Kennedy's mother
explaining why she cannot attend a social gathering:
"I've got a new maid and I'm doing the rough work now!"

Such stories do point up the main defect of equality—
that everyone wants it with their superiors! But there are
also critics of the American idea, who say: "No man can
be created equal. Ask any doctor. Some are born strong,
others weak. Many people are color-blind and some spiritually. A goodly number of any country's population are
stupid, others acquire stupidity. A comparative few are
born with wit, and for each of these there are one hundred
perfect fools. No one has a complete right to liberty, which
can be forfeited for certain good reasons. If we are all born
equal, equality ends at birth!"

From this point of view, it looks as if God must have
been born in Monte Carlo, but it also makes one think of
the eternal struggle of misfitting people these days, who
are constantly trying to impress those with superior ability
their concept of equality. While much is being done to ex-
tend the cultural opportunities so as to eliminate the causes
of certain inequality, not many take advantage of it. Night
schools are open to all for cultural improvement, and these
people should realize that social stratification is merely
another form of free enterprise competition. Even if someone does not possess the absorptive power to learn culture,
they can improve their personalities with the cultivation

of winning manners, a form of charm all can learn. The most touching and disarming grace of a human being comes from the heart.

No one would deny that America must be multi-racial. How the Colored Question can be solved to the satisfaction of all is a problem for which no one has yet come up with a solution. No one can deny that there are some colored who are better than whites, and also *vice versa*. And those colored people we dislike are surely those we would like no better if they wore white faces. I know several Afro-Americans who are just as selective as to whom they admit to their circle as I am my own. Social prejudice will be eventually outgrown but it can never be repealed by Act of Congress, unfortunately. Total integration is bound to come, but let us not forget that the mills of God grind slowly. Meanwhile, America needs the Negroes and the Negroes need America.

Politicians have a way of kicking the football of one issue too hard, or so hard that it remains out of sight until a catastrophe occurs. Happily, as this book goes to press there seems a concerted move to act on the population "explosion." Experts predict that "standing room only" will be our lot if it continues at the present rate of increase. One person for every square foot of the Earth's surface is the logical outcome in one thousand years from now— if the birthrate keeps apace. Even at today's figure the total number of persons living equal approximately the total number that ever lived prior to the year 1900! Demographic experts insist that if the situation goes unchecked by 1980 California will have no vacant coast space anywhere; and cities like Tucson and Phoenix in Arizona will

have to become one. In 1910 there were only ten cities in
the world with a population over one million; now there
are sixty!

Of course "standing room only" will never occur. Nature
will find a way, probably painful in the extreme, of pre-
venting it. Uncontrolled numbers inevitably build up to
a terrifying crash. We must listen to the teachings of
Eugenics, which stresses the need to bring into the world
only so many souls as it can safely hold.

No matter how democratic we become, there will always
be the need for masters and men under them, and I ask
myself: do our Congressmen try to serve two masters—
the party organization and the particular economic group
for whose interests they are committed? Are they doing
all they can to prevent our natural riches from being used
up through folly or vested interests? Are some Americans
swayed too much by their internal propaganda so they do
not vote and act from innermost convictions?

I am well aware that, as a writer, I am supposed only
to witness and record—not to pass moral judgment. As I
have said before, I have no quarrel with automation or
materialism. I simply believe that there are other ends
to life that are as important. I'm sure many a reader
wonders how long the U.S.A. will go on playing the playboy of the Western World by financing it and thus pre-
venting it from putting its own house in economic order.
We have, among other things, turned Germany into a
Champagne-bibbing nation, but have we enhanced the
character of its people?

I believe it is true that for all the noisy extreme leftists
and rightists in most countries there are many more silent
moderates who feel the middle of the road is the best way

of keeping out of a rut. We must try to avoid what the poet Tennyson called the "falsehood of extremes." The Golden Mean, as the Greeks termed moderation, should be our aim. In this regard the Space race will have to come to terms with common sense eventually.

Opinions on these matters of moment will differ, just as American temperament differs throughout the land, like the threading of its many rivers. In spite of the bromide that America is a melting pot, I always doubt that we are as homogeneous a people as some observers say. It seems a healthy situation that immigrants keep up their picturesque traditional ethnic ceremonies after becoming citizens. In no wise can these simple expressions detract from a sense of loyalty. Soon enough a composite culture will come to terms with all the differing environments. Our free-wheeling system of letting things develop by themselves will take care of this.

Because I am an idealist, who is convinced that all ideals of youth come true (usually when the idealist ceases to be young!), I believe the present debased taste for Art and Literature will finally be laughed away. The time will come when the untalented will no longer succeed in creating the incomprehensible—and the disingenuous will find it no longer possible to pass it off onto the gullible! We shall eventually have to stop cheapening ourselves by pretending to enjoy the pornographic. Thousands of people do not attend the theater because they are bored to death by it. I am basing these predictions on the fact that man's mind is as viable as he is himself. History shows that, on more than one occasion, the time when he seemingly lost all sense of morality witnessed the birth of an entirely new morality.

At the present time genius is undervalued and mere talent overpraised. Today, paid press agency brings mediocrity into greater prominence than it would otherwise enjoy. Perhaps it is just as well that we cannot accurately measure a man until he has been dead for a while. It is a lot better than the vulgar journalism which proclaims in every innovator a sign of genius. Americans are deprived of many artistic delights because of stern box office demands!

In the case of true genius, it is always difficult to explain what it is in any one of them that entitled them to that designation. I, for instance, think that the late Tadé Styka, the Polish-American portraitist, could confer a mood of immortality on his sitters in a manner similar to Titian. In poetry, I have always felt that Harold Pulsifer could versify regional humanity as well as Kipling. And I insist that Edward MacDowell is still America's greatest composer, old-fashioned though he may seem to others. His time will come again.

It is peace, not war, that brings changes in attitudes—and to its paradox we must not only ascribe changes in taste but also a slump in moral values, which has increased the crime rate since the war ended. Freedom is ever fraught with danger and many today are victims of American freedom! But there is already a sign of a change—that most permanent of forces in America. The true soil of America, on which its idea first took root, will grow again a larger generation of those who care for the things of lasting value. Those who do not believe in any belief at all have almost had their day, and I am sure everyone who thinks is anxious that the idolization of trivial people will also end.

Troubles will always be with us and will continue to spring up in all parts of the world. We shall have to expect the usual share of blame when the world does not spin 'round the way it ought to spin. We may be, for all I know, doomed to be perpetually misunderstood by the rest of the world, save for the perceptive few. Even so, it is better to be understood by a handful than none at all!

But we live in decidedly apocalyptical times. There is a machine of massive electronic proportions under construction by American specialists which may bring about a war-proof world in a decade or so. And I read lately about the Nuclear Neutralization Pact, suggested by Robert Dentler and Phillips Cutright, which could solve our worries about the Bomb. When we reflect on the harvest of incredible inventions, something new only has to be envisioned by a genius, and its fruition may change the entire world overnight. Poor, wonderful, maligned Twentieth Century! Everyone ought to be thrilled to be a part of it.

And the road ahead? It should be clear enough, but here is a lovely allegory from Irish folklore that illumines it for me. A traveler on horseback years ago was trying to find the right road to Dublin, that city which has been a fickle mistress for many an Irishman. Passing a peasant, he drew his rein and asked the way. But the man wrinkled his brow, as if puzzled. "I'm sorry, Sir," he replied with courtly courtesy, "I do not know the road to Dublin. But those who come from the direction in which you are going, tell me of its wonders and its terror."

International misunderstandings are far more dangerous than disagreements. We must try to close as much as we wisely can the rift between the East and West. I believe the best approach would be in happy measure between the spirit of the conservative Washington and the liberal Lincoln, who would want us to bridge the gap between the forward and the backward nations. This should be done by helping them to help themselves.

Individually we have all got to raise ourselves to full stature, remembering Emerson's advice that being a good citizen means putting one's soul into it. We ought frequently to remind ourselves that freedom is never offered at a bargain; it is always dearly bought. Never should any American conform to whatever course he feels is wrong. Whenever you get angry about the way things are going, you should never hesitate to write to your Congressman —or even to the President himself. It should ever be remembered that it is part and parcel of greatness to be wrong sometimes. Abraham Lincoln, and many other important men of the day, protested our early war with Mexico, but their protests went unheeded. The future proved them to have been right.

We hold our destiny in our own hands, and facing it squarely we shall make our heritage safe for ourselves and our children. Ponder the advice of that great American, Theodore Roosevelt, who said these many years ago: "Nine tenths of wisdom is in being wise in time. And if a people let the time for wise action pass, it may bitterly repent."

Rosoff Hotel
New York (36)
   Jan.-June 1963.